"Captivating. Heart-stopping. Soul-searching. Honest. Challenging. All of these words describe *Letters from My Father's Murderer*. As the mother of a convicted murderer, I understand the painful process of writing out of the depths of raw emotions, combined with the goal of using the truth to help set people free. If you long to understand and experience true forgiveness, don't miss this book. It will give you renewed hope, fresh faith, and a platform upon which you can build redemption, restoration, and a new kind of normal."

CAROL KENT, speaker and author of *When I Lay My Isaac Down*

"I stand amazed! As I finished this book about the journey of a daughter seeking to forgive her father's killer, I was overwhelmed at the mercy and grace of God who transformed not only the daughter but the murderer as well. *Letters from My Father's Murderer* examines the darkness within all of our hearts and exposes how light can shine brightly, even in the darkest places, when we seek to find the truth. The real truth. Whether we live in suburbia or peek through twelve-foot barbed wire fences to the outside world, the power of Jesus can set us free."

TAMMY WHITEHURST, motivational speaker and founder of Joy for the Journey

"There is no easy fix for life's most devastating circumstances. I'm grateful to Laurie Coombs for finding the courage to share from the heart about her loss and how her newfound faith in God gave her the strength to endure. If you are currently facing uncertainty or the unthinkable—I encourage you to pick up a copy of *Letters from My Father's Murderer* and be encouraged. Truly!"

RENEE FISHER, author of *Forgiving Others, Forgiving Me*

"Laurie is a living, breathing example that God does work all things together for good to those who love Him and surrender their lives, their hurts, and their circumstances to Him. In *Letters from My Father's Murderer*, Laurie invites the reader to journey with her through her pain, her confusion, her questions, and her anger toward the man who murdered her father, and the transforming process God led her through to find true forgiveness and ultimate peace. . . . Through it all, she is now able to take the blessings which God so graciously poured out to her as she kept her eyes on Him throughout her journey, and to bring them forth to bless others and encourage them in their journey of forgiveness, of trusting God, and of surrendering all to Him. It is a shining testimony that nothing is impossible with God and that Jesus came to redeem mankind to Himself. His desire is to set you free! If you have been wounded and struggle with forgiveness, this book is for you. It is truly transformational."

KRISTIE CALDER, founder of TRANS4MATION Ministries, speaker, and certified professional life coach

"This is a story of redemption, forgiveness, and reconciliation. Truthfully, I could not put the book down. I found Laurie's vulnerability, authenticity, and rawness refreshing. I know that this book will lead many to God's grace, not only to learn forgiveness, but to find forgiveness. Read this book carefully; you will probably discover some lies buried in your own heart."

DAN FRANK, lead pastor of Grace Church, Reno, Nevada

"In *Letters from My Father's Murderer*, Laurie Coombs weaves an intriguing true story—one that captivated me from page one. This story of forgiveness, redemption, restoration, and repentance is full of real and raw emotion that brings the reader to understand their own need for forgiveness or for extending forgiveness. Though not all of us have experienced the horror of losing a loved one to murder, we all deal with our own dark corners of the heart. Laurie's motives for extending forgiveness and looking through the 'lens of the gospel' will echo in my heart for many moments to come."

SARAH FRANCIS MARTIN, author of *Just RISE UP!*

"When you are a pastor, people come into your office seeking advice. You can only hope that what you offer and the small part you play will be used to the glory of God and for their joy. In these pages, you have just that. It didn't come easy or without struggle but Laurie has penned her journey of forgiveness in hopes that it can help you do the same, to the glory of God and for your joy."

BOBBY GROSSI, pastor of Living Stones Church, Reno, Nevada

LETTERS *from*
MY FATHER'S MURDERER

LETTERS *from*
MY FATHER'S MURDERER

A JOURNEY OF FORGIVENESS

LAURIE A. COOMBS

Kregel
Publications

For Jesus.
For Mom and Dad.
For Travis.
And for my amazing children.
I love you.

The night is far gone; the day is at hand.
So then let us cast off the works of darkness
and put on the armor of light.
                                    Romans 13:12

Contents

Preface

As I sat across from my dad at a local restaurant, he said to me, "Laurie, when I die, I want people to remember me for who I am. I don't want anyone turning me into something I'm not." It was an unusual comment. Enough to make me rest my overstuffed fajita on the plate in front of me and stare at him in bewilderment. I wasn't quite sure how to respond, so I didn't.

"It's just that, when someone dies," Dad continued to explain after a moment, "people only want to talk about the good parts of that person. But that's not who they really are. There are good parts and bad parts to every one of us."

Admittedly, as strange as the comment was, I thought my dad had a point. But I don't think either one of us knew the significance of those words when spoken. Neither one of us knew what was to come. My dad did not know when he was going to die.

But a month later, he did. Abruptly. Unexpectedly. Tragically. My dad was murdered. And that conversation we had over dinner was engraved upon my heart.

I tried to honor his request. His words weighed heavy upon my heart as I wrote his eulogy a few days after his death, and each time I spoke about his life and death, his words resounded in my mind. But still, the significance of those words eluded me for many years. It wasn't until I began to write this book—as I began to share my story publicly—that I knew why those words were spoken. I knew then, without a doubt, that the Holy Spirit encouraged my dad to speak those words to me, over a decade before I needed them, to give me the freedom to write what I have to say here.

Now, I must tell you, throughout this book I share many difficult, intimate details about my dad's murder, but this story is not ultimately about the circumstances behind my dad's death. Its intent is not to sensationalize sin or murder in any way. I honestly think our culture does entirely way too much of that as it is, and the thought of contributing to this unhealthy fascination repulses me.

No. Instead, this book is about redemption. It tells the crazy, messy story of a baby Christian having witnessed enough of God's grace to follow Jesus into the depths of her darkness, knowing good would ultimately prevail. It's the story of two enemies willing to trust God enough to walk down a path neither one wanted to enter.

This book is about learning true forgiveness.

It's about learning to love your enemies.

It's about trading bitterness for joy.

It's about freedom.

It's a book about the grace, mercy, healing, forgiveness, and redemption that can only be given by Jesus. But ultimately, it's a story that displays the glory of our God.

I never thought it possible to see any good come out of my past, let alone to see good emerge out of my dad's murder. That's not to say I abandoned all my hopes and dreams, but I had mistakenly thought any good in my future would result in spite of my past, not *as a result of it.* But I had grossly underestimated the grace of God.

You see, God loves us. He is with us, whether we recognize His presence or not. He is intimately acquainted with the inner workings of our lives. He knows what we've been through. He knows our sorrows. He knows our greatest hopes and dreams. And what never ceases to amaze me is that God continually holds His hand out toward us, beckoning us to come and receive all He has to offer despite our unruly hearts.

God has not left us to sit in our pain. Jesus came to heal. He is our redeemer, and I know it is His desire to lift each of us out of our despair and bring us in—to a new, better place. A place rich in beauty and blessings.

But I must confess. The path toward redemption isn't easy, and it's certainly not pretty. It requires us to lay ourselves down before God. To take His commands seriously. To not only read the Bible and agree with its precepts in thought, but to *do* the Word of God. To do whatever it is God calls us to do, even when it doesn't make much sense at the time. Even when it means we must sacrifice our will for His. This, my friend, is where redemption begins. The moment we lay down our fear, our pride, and our resistance—the moment we say yes to God—we begin to experience life as He intended, the life Jesus died for us to have.

A life marked by grace.

Now, I know my story is not an easy one to embrace, but I believe it has the power to transform lives. I have witnessed God do the impossible. I have seen Him redeem a situation that seemed without hope or purpose. He has brought good out of evil, love out of hate, and peace out of despair. God has truly worked all things for good in my life. And I believe with all my heart that He will do that for you as well, if you let Him.

I pray you will.

Thank you for entering into this journey with me. For giving me the privilege to speak into your life. It is an honor not taken lightly.

Note: In writing this book, I tried to re-create the events, locales, and conversations to the best of my ability from my memories of them. Due to the highly sensitive nature of this story, I have changed the names of some individuals involved to protect their identity and privacy.

Introduction

I was nearing a major transition in my life. A transition I had looked forward to for many years. Summer had come. With one more semester finished and only two more left before college graduation, I could hardly contain my excitement. I was so close to the time when I'd finally be able to spread my wings and experience all life had to offer. To the time when I'd be on my own. When I could start my career and marry the man I loved.

It seemed my life was finally about to begin.

Travis and I had been dating for nearly three years at this point—all of which were long distance. He was part of my plan. Part of what I looked forward to, and I could hardly wait for the day when our good-byes would be a thing of the past.

It was hard saying good-bye to one another over and over again; but for that summer, we wouldn't have to. Travis was coming home from the university he was attending, and I was practically giddy with excitement. The prospect of being able to spend three whole months in the same city was just about as thrilling as anything could have been.

He ended up working for my dad's construction company when he got back. This arrangement wasn't planned. It just sort of worked out that way, and I was glad it did. My dad had come to know Travis as much as he could over the years, but he didn't really know him. So I liked the idea of them spending more time together. I thought it was about time they became better acquainted.

We saw a lot more of Dad than usual at that time. The two of them working together provided opportunity and motivation for me to come around a bit more. I lived some thirty-plus miles away from the site where they worked, but I made sure to stop by for lunch or to drop off some Big Gulps every once in a while as an excuse to see them. It was kind of nice having the two most important men in my life together all the time. They really did seem to like one another, and that made me happy.

Outside of work, Travis and I were practically inseparable. It was a little ridiculous, I must say. We just couldn't seem to get enough of one another and were so tired of being apart that we felt we had to make the most of our time together. But Dad and I did do our own thing every now and again. In fact, I invited my dad to take me out to dinner one night when Travis was busy with his family. I did that a lot back then, and Dad always eagerly took me up on it. He seemed to relish every opportunity I gave him to see me.

We talked about a lot of things that night, but one part of our conversation in particular struck me. My dad told me about a woman he'd been dating. He said she was "a good Christian woman." I know it's normal for a lot of people to say things like that, but it wasn't for my dad. Not once had I heard him label someone a "good Christian." Quite honestly, I don't think he gave much importance—or thought, for that matter—to being a Christian at all, up to this point. That's just not who my dad was.

Dad didn't say much about this woman, but he did tell me a little. He seemed smitten. He lit up as he talked about her and the new direction she seemed to be pointing him toward. "I've been going to church again," he told me.

"Oh," I said, a bit surprised.

"And I've been reading the Bible, too."

"Really?" I asked. No one in my family read the Bible, especially my dad. Growing up, we had a Bible in the house, but it was the pristine white, hard leather kind you set on display and never pick up.

He continued to talk. To be honest, I don't remember all he said, but I do remember it had a lot to do with Jesus. And I didn't get it. I smiled and nodded as he spoke, trying to be polite, while thinking, *Whatever's going to make you happy, Dad.* I wasn't trying to be condescending or anything like that. It's just that I had dismissed religion as some elaborate hoax years before. But I had to admit, as I listened to my dad speak about God, he seemed happy. And I wanted him to be happy. I wanted him to find peace in this life—a peace that seemed to escape him ever since his own dad died close to six years before—and if this Jesus thing would ultimately help him, then I was for it. Though admittedly, I didn't quite understand it.

I began to notice subtle changes in my dad after that. He never did talk to me about his faith again, but I saw it in his actions. It was nothing crazy, but there definitely was something different about him.

My dad took us houseboating on Lake Powell toward the end of that summer. A bunch of us ended up going. Travis came along, of course, as did my sister and her family. My Aunt Patsy and Uncle Rick were there with their sons as well.

It was a fun vacation. We spent the week waterskiing, wakeboarding, and tubing. We went swimming and rock jumping. We explored some of the Native American ruins, seeing petroglyphs from days of old. And we also spent quite a bit of time just hanging out with one another, talking or playing board games.

Most of our time that week was spent together, and I liked that, but as the week was coming to an end, I kind of wanted to steal away a bit of time with my dad. While the others were busy doing something else, I motioned to my dad, asking him to take Travis and me out on the boat. He hesitated for a moment and seemed to wonder whether he should invite the rest of the crew, but I quickly mouthed, "No. Let's just go." And we did.

Travis was wakeboarding behind the boat while Dad drove and I watched—ready to hold my orange flag high to tell other boaters to watch out for him if he fell. I smiled as I watched Travis, and I'm not quite sure if the look on my face betrayed the depth of my feelings for him or if my dad was simply thinking about all the time he'd spent with Travis himself that summer, but out of nowhere, my dad said, "I know you're going to marry that guy, and I just want you to know that I approve."

"What?" I asked, shifting in my seat. Travis and I had not broached the subject with Dad yet.

He looked at me. "I just want you to know that I think he's a really good guy."

"He is a good guy," I said.

"I really like him."

"Thanks, Dad," I said, feeling a bit awkward. "I really like him, too." Dad stared at me with a knowing smile for a few moments before I playfully pushed him and said, "Okay, stop being weird." And we both laughed.

The rest of the week went by in a blur, and before we knew it, we were packing up.

Dad was headed home, but we weren't. We had a wedding to go to the following weekend in San Diego, so Travis and one of my cousins and I figured it was a good opportunity to take a road trip.

I didn't want my dad to drive all fourteen hours alone. I felt kind of bad for him, so I rode in his truck to where our routes separated, with Travis and my cousin Jeremy following behind. I don't remember exactly where we were when Dad pulled over to let me out. It was just some dry, dusty little town somewhere in southern Utah. But I do remember receiving one of those great big bear hugs my dad always gave me, as Travis pulled up behind us. Standing there beside the highway, my dad told me he loved me. I thanked him for our trip. And we unknowingly said our final good-bye.

Chapter 1

CAST INTO DARKNESS

I had always thought the world was a beautiful place, a place full of love and joy and light. I was dazzled by life, completely taken by its beauty. But just as I was coming into my own, just as I was about to embark on this thing called life—the very thing that captivated and excited me—I caught my first real glimpse of evil. The unthinkable happened and, for the first time in my life, I became intimately acquainted with the depths of human depravity. It broke my heart. It seemed all the beauty I'd once discovered was simply a veil masking the dark realities of life and, with that veil removed, the only thing left to see was darkness and pain and suffering.

What is wrong with this world? I wondered. *What is wrong with people?*

Aunt Patsy and Uncle Rick were standing in the light of their porch, waiting for Travis and their son, Jeremy, and me as we pulled up to their house in the darkness of early morning. We had driven all night after the wedding in San Diego through some of the most desolate parts of the California and Nevada desert. I had felt something the night before. I didn't know something bad had happened, but I had felt something. Something I cannot even begin to explain. It seemed my spirit knew what my mind had not yet been told, and all I knew was that I needed to be home.

Before getting out of the car, I paused for a moment to watch my aunt and uncle briefly from a distance. The call we had received sometime in the middle of the night asking us to come to their house had left the three of us feeling uneasy, and the sight of them on that porch only increased the feeling. They seemed anxious—deeply troubled—and that scared me. I love these two people dearly, but I didn't want to see them this time. Not under these circumstances. But as they began walking toward the car, I figured I had no other option but to get out and meet them, and so I did.

The darkness seemed to press in on me as I followed Jeremy up the familiar steps toward his parents' house. Travis trailed behind. "What's going on?" Jeremy asked nervously. The question was left unanswered, perhaps not even heard by his parents, who were both looking past him to me. Aunt Patsy stared at me as I drew near, with brows furrowed and sorrow so deep in her eyes that I could not even begin to understand the depth of pain she was feeling. Tears rolled freely down her cheeks, revealing a truth I did not want to know. And in that moment, I sensed the pain I saw in her eyes would soon become my own.

Shaking my head, I adamantly whispered, "No, no, no, no, no," through my tears.

Travis came near, and I grabbed his arm a bit too tight, I imagine, as my mind began to spin out of control. It was my dad. I knew it.

"Laurie, come inside," my aunt said softly, interrupting my thoughts. I hesitated.

I didn't want to go in. I didn't want to hear what they had to say. All I wanted was to run away. To pretend this wasn't happening. To pretend my life was no different than it was the day before, but I couldn't. I couldn't ignore what was happening. I couldn't go back. I couldn't change any of it. I knew that, and so when Travis gently urged me to go in a moment later, I did. Though every part of me was screaming inside, I unwillingly walked in and sat in an armchair in the family room to receive news that I knew would most assuredly crush my spirit and change the course of my life forever.

I don't remember how my aunt and uncle began the conversation. I'm sure they cushioned the blow somehow, but all I remember were the words, "Your dad was murdered last night. He's dead."

Travis was holding my hand, and I think I just about crushed it. I was stunned. Completely and totally taken aback. I thought maybe Dad had gotten in a car accident or been hit by a drunk driver or something. But murder? How was that even possible? We lived in a nice, quiet small town. We had a good family. We were honest, good people. How could my dad have been murdered?

"The man who killed your dad is in custody," I remember them saying as a storm raged in my mind. "He admitted to the murder. His name is Anthony Echols."

Anthony Echols. I knew that name. My dad had spoken to me about this man a month before. *That guy is suicidal,* I thought. *He left a note threatening suicide a while back. Why didn't he just kill himself? Why would he kill Dad when he could have just killed himself?* The thought played in my mind over and over until it came screaming out of my mouth. "Why the hell didn't he just kill himself?" I cried out with a few added expletives, as tears ran down my face.

And then I think I just about lost it.

I didn't quite know what to do with myself after that. I felt trapped, weighed down by a reality I could not accept. I could not accept the fact that my dad was gone. Taken by a senseless murderer. Snuffed out like the flame of a candle, just like that. I wanted to lash out. I wanted to scream. I wanted to hit something, throw something. I was so totally and completely full of anger and hatred that it nearly consumed me. And as I sat there in that chair, I felt a tidal wave of grief overtake every part of my soul, as I came to know intimately the pain I had seen in my aunt's eyes only moments before.

I don't know how long we stayed at my aunt and uncle's house. I don't remember much of anything that happened right after I was told, but I do know that Travis and I ended up down the street at my mom's house sometime later that morning. No one was there. My mom and her husband, Gary, were still on their way home from the wedding, which suited me just fine. I needed to process the whole thing for a while before I talked to anyone else, even my mom.

I stood in the middle of the living room in a fog. I didn't know what to do. I didn't know where to go from there. I wondered how I'd be able to return to a life that even remotely resembled something normal after what had happened. And as I stared off into the distance, I was struck by just how different everything looked. The whole world seemed to have changed around me. It was light outside by this time, but even the light of day seemed to have grown dim.

Travis and I lay down to try to get some rest. I closed my eyes, hoping to escape the nightmare that had become my reality, but it seemed my thoughts only grew louder in the stillness of that room. Tears escaped through fluttering eyelids, soaking the pillow beneath my head as I wrestled through the pain. I thought about my dad. About what he must have gone through the night before, and it simply tore me up. I wondered if he knew he was going to die. If he was scared. If he died quickly or suffered a slow death. And then it hit me. "He's gone," I whispered to myself. The full weight of what had happened pressed in on me. *I'll never be able to see my daddy again*, I thought sobbing uncontrollably. *I'll never have the chance to say good-bye. Or tell him I love him. He's gone. He's gone forever.*

I didn't know if what I was asking was even possible but, with eyes closed and hands tightly clutched around the sheet covering me, I silently pleaded with my dad to show himself one last time. I had heard stories of people coming in spirit to their loved ones moments after their death, and I wanted that. I desperately wanted to see my dad one last time. I wanted to know that he was okay. That he was in a better place. So I implored the heavens and begged my dad for a vision. I spent hours, it seemed, silently pleading, *Please . . . please show yourself . . . please*, until I fell silent in exhaustion.

I never did get what I asked for, and I'd be lying if I told you I wasn't disappointed about that, but as I lay perfectly still in that bed, no longer able to plead or cry or think, I did feel something. Even as an unbelieving skeptic, I could not deny the very real, peaceful presence in the room with us that morning. I couldn't explain it, and I certainly did not know what it was, but I felt it. And Travis did, too.

Mom came home a little later, just in time to help us field calls from reporters. None of us had done anything like this before, and we really didn't know what we were doing, but we tried our best, pushing our way through with a sense of duty and a desire to honor my dad. That first day was a long, terrible day. And as it came to a close, we all sat together in front of the TV to watch the news through dry, bloodshot eyes.

My family and I tried to pick up the pieces after that. Mark and Sheri—my brother and sister—and I were the heirs to Dad's estate. We were all in our early twenties at that time, entirely too young to be dealing with all that entailed, especially under these circumstances. And while I can't speak for my brother or sister, I certainly did not feel equipped to be doing what we were doing, so I welcomed all the help my mom and extended family offered. But there was still plenty we had to do on our own.

Here's the thing. After a normal death, there are wills, trusts, probate, distribution of property, and a funeral to arrange, but when someone is murdered, it's a different story altogether. On top of all that normal stuff, there are countless meetings with the DA, preliminary hearings, and a trial to deal with. But with all that aside, I think the most difficult thing I had to endure was the day Dad's house was released back to my family and me.

My dad had been murdered in his home and several days later, after the investigation was complete, it was time to take ownership of the property. I didn't want anything to do with it. I hated the very thought of having to deal with that place, but we had no choice. The house was legally ours.

Most people don't really think about this, but crime scenes are not cleaned up by the sheriff's department. They're given back to the legal owner just as they're found. I'm not sure if that's the case across the board, but that certainly was our experience. And let me tell you: that was a pretty awful thing to deal with.

The prospect of going to that place was daunting. I knew it was going to be ridiculously difficult for me to go into the house. To see the place Dad died. But I also knew that I needed to face the reality of what happened. And I figured if I didn't deal with it, others would be forced to deal with it in my stead.

Travis and I, along with my mom and brother, drove over to the house the day it was to be given back to us. As we pulled up, we saw several of my uncles carrying a bloodstained couch out of the house. I watched them for a moment, then turned away quickly as they loaded it into the bed of a truck headed for the dump. My uncles had apparently received permission from the sheriff's department to show up a bit early to remove a few things before we came so we wouldn't have to deal with them. They were there to carry part of our burden. I didn't know they were going to do that, but I was grateful they did.

Dad's camper was still loaded on his truck from our Powell trip. His boat was parked next to it. It seemed my dad hadn't even had the chance to fully unpack, and that made me sad. I stared at that camper for a moment and thought about all the fun things I had done with my dad growing up. About all the camping trips and the times we spent out on a lake somewhere. So many wonderful memories came to mind and, as I thought of them, I simply couldn't believe they were over. I thought I had so much more time with my dad, but time had run out.

As we got out of the car, Travis grabbed my hand tight and held it close to his body. I was thankful to have him there. He hadn't left my side since we had heard the news several days before, and I don't think he did until fall semester began later that month.

Some of the deputies on the case were standing on the front lawn, waiting for the appropriate time to approach us. My mom and brother walked up to them first; Travis and I slowly followed. I can't begin to explain how I felt in that moment, out in front of that house. No words can capture the full range of emotions. I was terrified, literally trembling with fear, as I looked at that house and thought about what I'd see inside.

I didn't really want to go in there, but I felt like I needed to face it, though I wasn't sure I'd make it through unscathed.

"Are you sure you want to go in there?" I heard Mom ask. She looked concerned. She hated that her children had to go through this whole mess.

"Yeah," I said.

I walked into the garage with Travis, behind Mom and Mark, looking for signs of anything out of the ordinary before going into the house. I seemed to have unintentionally taken on the role of detective, carefully noting every detail as I went. I wanted Anthony put away for life, and so I slowly and carefully searched every corner of that house to ensure nothing was missed.

The house was relatively clean except for the place the couch had been. My uncles had done their best to protect us but, even with the couch gone, the bloodstained carpet gave evidence to what had taken place several days before. I turned away the moment I saw that crimson stain, hoping to protect my heart; but a moment later, I found myself staring at it, wishing things had turned out differently.

The funeral took place a day or so later. I remember standing in front of hundreds of people, looking out over a sea of faces blurred by my tears. My voice quavered as I spoke of my dad. I really did love that man, and I just couldn't believe I had to say good-bye. Mark and Sheri said a few words as well, as did a few other family members. When the service ended, we dutifully stood at the back of the church to greet those who had come.

"He's in a better place," I heard over and over from guests as they left. But I wasn't entirely convinced they were right. Quite frankly, I didn't know where my dad was, and I think that was the thing I struggled with most.

The hope of heaven is written on every human heart. No one wants to believe this life is all there is to it; but to me, all that stuff in the Bible just seemed too good to be true, like some fanciful fairy tale concocted to tickle our ears and make our hearts feel all warm and fuzzy inside.

I have to admit, as I wrestled with Dad's death, I wanted to believe. For the first time in my life, I wanted to believe in God because ultimately I wanted to believe that my dad was in that better place those people talked about. I was so utterly desperate to know that Dad was okay—that he was somehow still there. But no matter how much I wanted to believe, I couldn't. I saw no proof. And I certainly wasn't about to abandon sound reason in order to make myself feel better.

I walked to a nearby park after the funeral. Travis and my cousins thought I needed to get away from it all, and they were right. I tried to think of other things, but my mind was still spinning on all that had happened, trying to make sense of the whole mess.

Anthony was less than a mile away in a jail cell.

I thought of him.

I thought of my dad.

It all felt so meaningless. Like a waste.

"They say everything happens for a reason," I said aloud as I struggled through confusion and grief and anger, "but how could there be a reason for *this*?"

Nothing good can come out of this, I thought. *Nothing.*

Chapter 2

THE WILDERNESS

School began. Travis moved back to Chico, California, to finish his degree while I finished mine in Reno. I lived in a small apartment by the university, away from my family and all the mess so I might be able to pour myself back into my studies and finish my last year well. Quite a bit remained to be done at home. Mom and Mark dealt with the majority of the legal stuff pertaining to the estate. I helped with whatever needed to be done, but they took the lead, and I was glad they did.

One of my professors assigned Mary Shelley's *Frankenstein* that semester. Reading a fictional book like that just seemed so irrelevant and inconsequential in comparison to life's real issues, as did the rest of my schoolwork, but I still went through the motions and did what I was supposed to do. After the murder, I never could quite find the words to express how I felt, and even now, I cannot fully explain the depth of feelings in my heart back then, but as I read that book, I found one paragraph in particular that gave words to some of my unspoken thoughts:

> I need not describe the feelings of those whose dearest ties are rent by that most irreparable evil, the void that presents itself to the soul, and the despair that is exhibited on the countenance. It is so long before the

mind can persuade itself that [he], whom we saw every day, and whose
very existence appeared a part of our own, can have departed for ever—
that the brightness of a beloved eye can have been extinguished, and the
sound of a voice so familiar, and dear to the ear, can be hushed, never
more to be heard.

Never more to be heard, I thought. *Never more.* It was hard for me to
wrap my mind around the fact that I'd never be able to see or talk to
my dad again. Many times going about my day, I'd think, *Oh, I gotta
tell Dad about . . .* only to realize he wasn't there to tell. Driving around
town, I'd catch a glimpse of a man in a truck, and for a brief moment
I'd wonder, *Was that Dad?*—knowing full well the absurdity of the
thought.

Grief does crazy things to the mind. You know the facts. You know
what happened, but you don't want to believe it. You want to believe
instead that what you just went through was all part of some crazy,
elaborate hoax that will come to an end at some point. That you'll wake
up one day to find it was all just a terrible nightmare.

*How is it that we live here on this earth and then, when we die, we
simply cease to exist?* I thought. *How is it that Dad was once here but is
now gone?* It was like a riddle, one I felt I could never solve. Now, I'm an
extremely rational person—I rationalize and analyze things to a fault—
and though I was able to rationally understand the finality of death, I
could not make sense of it. Thoughts spun around in my head without
relief. *What's the point of all this? Why are we even here?* I wondered.

I was angry, mostly with Anthony, but it was more than that. My
anger began the moment I was told of Dad's death, but as I watched
continuing news coverage of the murder, my anger only grew. I knew the
indifference I had felt in my own heart when watching other accounts
of tragedies. But this story was different. This story was about *my* dad.
And I knew others were watching with the same lack of concern and
disinterest I had felt over other tragedies. Perhaps they'd mutter "that's

too bad" to themselves, but moments later they would forget Dad's death altogether and go about their lives as usual. But I wasn't able to go about my life as usual. This *was* my life. This *was* my reality. A reality I could not escape. A reality that was not fair.

I couldn't do the things I did before the murder. I stopped watching TV, I turned off the news, I carefully screened movies to protect myself from seeing any type of violence, and, of course, the rap music I once listened to was definitely out. I just couldn't take it. All around me, throughout most of our culture, I saw an unhealthy fascination with murder. Rappers glorifying it. Television shows depicting it to boost ratings. Movies using it to entice audiences. Kids running around saying, "I'm going to kill you!" like it's no big thing. And old ladies sitting in the heat of summer, saying, "It's murderously hot in here." We have murder-mystery dinner parties. Murder-mystery board games. True crime TV shows. And most recently, someone was even callous enough to develop a murder reality show. We're glorifying it. Sensationalizing it. Because, after all, murder sells, right?

Seeing murder elevated to entertainment sickened me. I just wanted to scream, "This is not a game, people!" Murder is real. Murder is horrific. It is not entertainment. It is not something we should have this unhealthy fascination with. It's murder. Real people exist behind each and every murder. Real victims. Real families left behind. *Murder is not a game.* And it is certainly not something to be glorified.

I was a mess.

I tried not to be, but I was. I put a smile back on my face around others, and I think I had a lot of people fooled into thinking I was okay. But I wasn't. When I was alone, that smile would quickly fade, and I'd succumb to my pain and struggle with my grief. I'd clutch my teddy bear—a gift Dad had given me the Christmas before, a gift I thought I was entirely way too grown up to receive—and whisper, "Why . . . why did this have to happen?" as I lay on my tear-soaked pillow.

I really did miss him. I missed seeing the way he looked at me—the way only a father can look at his daughter with love and pride in his heart. I missed our silly conversations and the way we always seemed to poke fun at one another. But most of all I missed his great big bear hugs. I would have given just about anything to receive one more hug from my dad.

I wondered how long it would be before I began to forget. How long before I forgot the sound of his voice? The sound of his laugh? The way his eyes crinkled up in the corners when he smiled? All the quirky little things that made him who he was? I'd forget all that, eventually. And the thought of that just about pulled me under.

I cried for a long time. I let myself grieve. But after a while I decided it was time to move on. I didn't think my dad would have wanted me to continue on like that, and so I stopped crying and stopped allowing myself to be so angry. I knew I couldn't change my past and figured it was time to stop allowing my emotions to dictate my future.

Travis and I got married after graduation. It had been a little more than a year since Dad died, and I was finally starting to see some joy come into my life again.

It was a beautiful wedding, just like I had always dreamed. Three hundred people gathered together in the Catholic church Travis and I grew up in to see us pledge our lives to one another. It was the same church where we had said good-bye to Dad the year before. It didn't make much sense for us to get married there. I wasn't a believer—I had written Catholicism and Christianity off years earlier—and Travis wasn't a practicing Catholic at the time either, but for whatever reason, it's what we decided to do.

Our wedding day was truly amazing. I was so excited to finally be able to give myself to the man I love. But I have to admit that it was a little bittersweet. As a daughter, I felt the loss of my dad most on my wedding day. At no other time was his absence felt so strongly. My dad was supposed to be there, but he wasn't. Instead, my mom and brother walked me down the aisle and gave my hand to Travis. And Uncle Rick, who was like a second father to me growing up, danced with me during the father-daughter dance at the reception, as many guests clung to one another and cried. Admittedly, parts of our wedding were undeniably sad, but it was still a wonderful celebration. We did have a lot of fun despite Dad's absence, just as he would have wanted.

After the wedding, Travis settled into his career as a project manager for a construction company, and I went on to receive my teaching certificate from a college in Lake Tahoe. One month after I finished the program, my family and I were notified by the district attorney that the state would finally be able to try Anthony's case.

It was January 2003, two and a half years after the murder. After being pushed back several times for various reasons, the trial was finally going to happen. I was glad to get it over with. That trial had been lingering over our heads far too long, and I wanted nothing more than to close that terrible chapter of my life and move on.

There was a chill in the air as we walked up those courthouse steps on the first day. I shivered, not knowing whether it was the cold or my nerves that shook me. I hated entering the building Anthony was in. I hated the fact that I'd have to see him. That we'd be in the same room every day for up to two weeks. I had only seen him one time before, at the preliminary hearing, but whenever I saw that man—whether in person or in the media—I always got this terrible feeling in the pit of my stomach. Hate and anger and disgust always seemed to rise up when I saw him.

Only a few other people were in the courtroom when we arrived. Mom and I sat on the hard wooden benches with my aunts, uncles, cousins, and grandparents, as well as several other family friends, waiting for the trial to start. There were quite a number of us, leaving hardly enough room for anyone else on our side of the room.

Anthony was ushered in a moment later, after everyone settled. He looked down as he walked, avoiding eye contact, and found his seat next to his attorney. My eyes filled with tears as I thought about what a mess that man had made of things.

The trial came into session. Opening arguments were given. The defense claimed that Anthony "didn't mean for this to happen." They said it was an accident. But the prosecution refuted those claims, arguing that Anthony "deliberately planned the murder."

Arguments went back and forth for almost two weeks, and emotions ran high as my family and I quietly listened to the proceedings. We felt intense rage hearing some of Anthony's claims, but we were also able to rejoice in many prosecution victories as well. It was ridiculously hard to be there—hearing slanderous claims against Dad, seeing graphic pictures we tried to ignore, and quite simply trying to keep it all together—but in the end, it was worth it.

The jury did not believe Anthony's story. All the lies had been weeded out, revealing the truth of what had really happened. This was no accident, as Anthony claimed. Anthony murdered my dad deliberately and was ultimately found guilty of first-degree murder and burglary.

Family members were given the opportunity to speak to the jury during the sentencing phase—in what was called a "Victim Impact Statement"—prior to determining Anthony's sentence. A few of us chose to take the stand and speak.

I was super nervous to get up there, but I wanted the court to know who my dad really was. Way too much slander had gone on during the trial in an effort to make Anthony's actions somehow justifiable, and so I thought it was about time we put all that nonsense to rest. My heart pounded as the judge called me to the witness chair. From there, I addressed the court, while Anthony watched and listened.

Tears ran hot down my cheeks as I spoke. I told the court that my dad was a flawed man—a man who had made many mistakes, just as we all do. But that he should not be defined only by his mistakes. I spoke of his love for those around him. I told them about the man who sat at my sister's bedside during her two brain surgeries, donating blood when she needed it. I told them about the man who was faithfully married to my mom for twenty-two years before he fell apart and left. The man who loved his children and would have done anything for us.

Anthony hung his head low as I spoke. He seemed sad, but I was undeterred. I wanted him to know what he had done. How he had destroyed my life and the life of my family. How he had robbed my future children of their grandpa. How his decision had left a wave of destruction behind, affecting many, many people. Something he most likely couldn't even conceive.

Anthony looked up and, for a brief moment, our gazes locked. A chill ran down my spine. I quickly averted my eyes and, with new-found resolve, I turned toward the jury—those commissioned to decide Anthony's fate, those responsible for ensuring justice would be done—and left them with a challenge:

> Until the day of Anthony's death, we will have to deal with the fact that there is a man out there who took our dad's life. How long this murderer will spend in prison is left up to you, and we encourage you to help our family in our pursuit of justice.
>
> This tragedy, which has affected all of our lives, is not over. This will be something we must live with for the rest of our lives; nonetheless, only when justice is served will we be able to move on with our lives and have closure.
>
> Leonardo da Vinci once said, "He who does not punish evil commends it to be done. Justice requires power, insight, and will. . . ." I challenge you to uphold justice and sentence Anthony to life imprisonment without the possibility of parole.

My heart was pounding as I finished my statement and returned to my seat.

The jury returned a little while later. Anthony was sentenced to two consecutive life terms without the possibility of parole. He was cuffed and taken away as my family and I rejoiced over the ruling. Justice had been served. It was over. And I'd finally be able to move on with my life.

With the trial behind us, Travis and I eagerly settled into our next season in life. My first teaching job began only days after the trial ended. Starting my new career seemed to mark a turning point in my life. It felt like I was finally past all the fallout from the murder, and things started to look a bit more normal.

I continued to teach for several years. But when Travis and I found out we were going to have a baby, we immediately began crunching numbers, trying to figure out how I might be able to stay home with our children. Quite honestly, it took a bit of figuring and certainly some financial sacrifice, but we ultimately made it work. I was so excited I could hardly stand it. I couldn't wait to be a mommy.

Everything seemed to be going well in the beginning of my pregnancy, but as it progressed, I started experiencing some pretty substantial complications. It ended up being an extremely high-risk pregnancy, one that involved six weeks of bed rest, quite a bit of pain, and countless trips to several doctors. And in the mix of all that, we were told there was absolutely no possible way we would have a "normal" child. At first they thought our baby girl had Down syndrome, then cystic fibrosis. But when all those tests came back negative, we were told she may not make it and, if she did, she'd most assuredly have some sort of problem.

Travis and I were absolutely devastated. We had already been through so much, and it just didn't seem fair to be dealing with more. My life was just starting to level out, and now this. *Why is there so much pain in this world?* I wondered. *Haven't I been through enough?*

I was desperate for my child. And I wasn't willing to accept what the doctors were telling me. They said she had no chance, but something inside me told me they were wrong. I had never prayed words out of my own heart before, but I figured if there was a time to pray, it was now.

And so I prayed to a God I did not know, a God I wasn't sure existed, and asked everyone else to pray alongside me. Whole church congregations held our little girl up in prayer. And despite all odds—despite what all the experts and specialists had told us—she was quite literally healed in utero before our eyes. As Travis and I sat in a cold, sterile doctor's office time and again over the course of several months, we watched God heal our little girl on an ultrasound monitor.

"It looks like it's going away," I'd tell my doctor, hoping he'd agree. But he never did.

"Laurie, don't do that to yourself," he'd say instead. "That's highly improbable."

And it was.

Months later our little girl, Gabrielle "Ella" Renée, was born. She was perfectly healthy, defying all sound logic. And despite my skepticism, I knew what had happened. I knew God had healed her. There was simply no other explanation.

"Where are you now with your faith?" my girlfriend Nicole gently asked a few months down the road. Nicole had been praying for me to come to Christ since we were fifteen, and I think she hoped all the pregnancy complications would get me there.

"Well," I said, "I used to question whether God was real, but now I know there is a God." That was as far as I could go at the time.

Our second daughter, Avery Grace, was born two years later, without complication. Having gone through all that stuff with Ella, we counted ourselves "lucky" to have two healthy, beautiful little girls. But, of course, I now know luck had nothing to do with it.

Life began to taste sweet once again, but I still had times of sadness. In quiet, sweet moments as I watched my little girls play with their daddy, it was as if I were looking into a mirror of my past. I'd see myself in them and my dad in Travis. Of course I'd always wish they had the chance to know their grandpa. He would have been a wonderful grandpa to them—it seemed they were cheated somehow. Like something precious had been stolen from them. Something they didn't even know was missing. So I had my moments, but overall, my life was good. Travis and I had finally found our sweet spot.

I certainly had been through quite a bit by this point, and it seemed to me that I had been the one who had gotten myself through it all. In my mind, I was resilient, strong, and capable of just about anything. The problem was, my strength was quickly becoming a major source of pride.

"I don't know how you do it, Laurie," some would say. "You've been through so much. You're such a strong person." And in my heart, I'd think, *I know. I am pretty amazing.* These comments were intended to be compliments, words to encourage me, but they only fueled my growing pride. And, as they say, pride most certainly does come before the fall.

I started noticing issues with my health little more than a year later. I was nauseous all the time, and I just didn't feel quite right.

"I think I'm pregnant," I told Travis.

"Really?"

"Yeah, but the tests keep coming back negative. Do you think I should get a blood test?"

Travis thought I was being silly, but I went to my doctor the next week anyway. He ended up being right. I wasn't pregnant, and the specialist I was referred to said my nausea was most likely caused by stress. The nausea went away after I took some medication. But then my heart started acting funny, and I began having headaches all the time. *Maybe something's really wrong with me,* I thought. And that was it. I was struck with fear at the idea, and no matter how many times I tried to persuade myself that I was just fine, I couldn't believe it.

After that, a new symptom seemed to show up almost daily. I was tired all the time—and I mean ridiculously tired. I felt dizzy. I started having digestive issues. I felt nervous and absentminded. But I think the worst part of all was that my mind didn't seem to work properly.

That scared me. I couldn't think clearly. My brain always seemed to be in a fog that left me feeling out of touch with reality and emotionally detached from others.

I was desperate to figure out what was wrong. I spent quite a bit of money going from doctor to doctor in search of a fix, only to be told I was experiencing the physical effects of anxiety that had built up over the years. Quite simply, there was no easy fix, and I was left with absolutely no idea about how I might be able to get better.

It didn't take much for me to lose hope at that point. And of course, that's when the depression hit. I tried desperately to fix myself—to pull myself out of that dark pit—but, for the first time in my life, I could not save myself.

I tried all that the world tells you to do in situations like this. I tried therapy. I tried eating better and exercising more. I tried meditation. I tried taking a stress management class. I tried yoga. I tried reading self-help books. I tried implementing those silly principles found in *The Secret*—the power of positive thinking. And I even considered going to a Buddhist retreat, if you can imagine that! I truly was desperate, but nothing helped.

I really don't like taking medication—I don't like things messing with my body—but at this point I figured I had no other options. I took an antidepressant at the advice of my doctor, hoping it would finally provide the relief I desperately needed, but after only a few days, I realized that the medication was yet another rabbit trail leading to false promises. The medication was short lived. It didn't work. In fact, it had only made things worse.

I felt like I had been plunged into the pit of hell. Anxiety raged like a storm within me, as my mind spun completely out of control. One irrational thought after another entered my mind, as if planted there by another, sending me into a tailspin of fear. I was terrified. My mind was so cloudy and unstable that I didn't know what I was capable of.

I don't think I was ever suicidal, but I do have to admit—a small part of me wanted to give up and die. I was terrified of dying. Truthfully, it was probably my greatest fear, but to die just seemed easier somehow. I felt so incredibly empty and alone. I had experienced so much pain, and that pain never seemed to stop. I wasn't sure life was worth all that pain. I desperately wanted to give up, but I couldn't. I was a wife and a mommy, and I didn't want to leave my children as Dad had left me. My family needed me, and because of that, I chose to fight.

But I couldn't solve this one on my own. I had no answers. I had finally come to the end of myself, and I needed help.

I called Sarah. She and I had become friends a couple years earlier, after meeting at a Gymboree class when our oldest were babies. We talked for a little while about nothing in particular, as I worked up enough courage and laid down enough pride to finally ask, "What church do you go to?"

"Oh, my church?" she asked, sounding a bit surprised. "It's called Grace."

The following Sunday, my family and I willingly walked through those church doors to attend a service for the first time since I was a teenager. I was terrified, but my desperation trumped my fear. All other options had been exhausted.

It seemed God was my last and only hope.

Chapter 3

THE LIGHT

I walked away from God when I was fifteen. It was the same year my parents divorced—the year I became a bit rebellious.

It was a tumultuous time for my family. My sister had gone through two brain surgeries within six months a few years before in an attempt to control her epilepsy. Mom and Dad had planned on only one surgery, but complications after the first necessitated the second. I think it just about killed Mom to watch her daughter go through this, and it certainly wasn't easy for Dad. It was kind of tense around our house at that time, and I'm pretty sure all that stress took its toll on their marriage.

My dad's dad died of cancer one year later, at the age of sixty-three. It was an aggressive cancer. Opa lost that battle before he even had a chance to fight. He was gone only months after his diagnosis. Dad had been close with Opa, and he took it hard.

My dad was just not the same after his dad died. He had always been a levelheaded, responsible man and a very present, loving father, but things changed after that.

"What's the matter?" Mom would ask. "Are you okay?"

"I'm just having a hard time getting over my dad's death," he'd reply. Mom asked the same questions over and over and was met with the same answer—"I'm just having a hard time with Dad's death." Then one morning, his answer changed.

"Are you okay?" Mom asked once again.

Instead of his usual answer, Dad said he thought he might be happier if they separated. Being truthful, he told her there was a woman he had become interested in, and he wanted to see where that would go.

Looking back, I think Dad was going through something similar to what I ended up going through years later. He seemed lost, depressed even. I honestly don't think my parents ever stopped genuinely loving one another, and their problems were certainly not insurmountable. But for whatever reason, my dad wasn't happy. After Opa died, I think my dad began to wonder why that was. And just as the whole thing started for me, I imagine a thought came to his mind, a lie —*Maybe it's my marriage*—and that was it.

Mom was blindsided. Their marriage wasn't perfect and there were certainly things they both could have worked on, but she had no idea this was coming. I think she tried to get Dad to stay, but his mind was clearly made up. He was leaving. She woke me that morning to tell me the news as Dad packed all his belongings. I was completely shocked. And as I sat on my bed trying to understand why all this was happening, my mom laid on my bedroom floor in a fetal position and sobbed uncontrollably.

Dad left without saying good-bye. It was pretty crummy. Mark and Sheri were still asleep when I saw him pack his truck and leave. I thought he was a coward for doing that. I don't think he would have had the heart to go through with it if he had to tell us himself, so he simply chose not to. And that one selfish act set him on a path of destruction that changed the course of our lives forever.

Divorce changes things. When Mom and Dad separated, our family dynamic shifted from a united whole naturally coming together to fragmented pieces drifting apart. It took effort to come together after that. Dad called frequently to try to see us, and I think my brother and sister were open to getting together, but I refused. I was angry with him. I wanted nothing to do with my dad, and I knew that tore him up.

Dad had always been there for me, but that changed when he left. Despite what most teenage girls say, a girl needs her daddy quite possibly more during this time than any other time in her life. This is a time of discovery, a time of newfound independence, and if a girl doesn't have her daddy at home to be her rock—showing her what a good man looks like, giving her proper male affection—she's going to seek it elsewhere. And I did.

I think I've always had a bit of a rebellious streak in me. I certainly don't blame any of my actions on my dad. I know I am solely responsible for my sins. But the moment Dad left was the very moment my rebellion really began. I wasn't trying to be rebellious. I wasn't feeling spiteful or anything like that. I just wanted to direct my own life, and so I rebelled—against my parents and against the religious system I was raised in.

As a Catholic, I had watched my siblings and several of my older cousins receive the sacrament of confirmation before me. I had gone through catechism and all the sacraments up to that point but, when it came time to get confirmed, I found myself asking many questions. *What am I doing?* I wondered. *What is confirmation anyway? Do I have to get confirmed? Isn't confirmation just another ritual?* I took my questions to my catechism teacher.

"What am I actually doing when I get confirmed?" I asked.

"Well . . ." she said, "you're confirming your faith."

"My faith in what?"

"Your faith in the Catholic Church," she replied.

I thought about that. Something about her response didn't seem quite right to me, and I'm not sure her response accurately reflects the position of the Roman Catholic Church. But of course I didn't know that at the time, so I said, "I don't think I'm ready to do that." A week or so later, I decided not to go through with confirmation. Mom was having a crisis of her own after Dad left, so she didn't argue with my decision.

Catholicism was all we had ever known, but after that Mom and I decided to explore other churches together. It felt like we were two Catholic girls who had jumped ship, and in my silly teenage mind, I felt kind of like a revolutionary of sorts, rejecting the system I had grown up in to search for something better.

Our search didn't last long. It ended rather quickly after visiting a few nondenominational churches that we didn't feel particularly drawn to. I continued to go to a youth group with a friend for a while after that, but then I started feeling convicted about some of the things I was doing. I didn't like that too much. Even then, I had this sense that I needed to be all in and that, if I continued to go to church, I would have to make some serious changes in my life. But I wasn't willing to do that.

So I walked away from God altogether.

I had never really known God, though. The god I had grown up with was a distant force who imposed rules on a people he couldn't possibly know or have time to care about. As a child, I was told about a god who simply expected us to follow rules—expected perfection, in essence—and if we failed, we were forced to talk to a priest about those sins when brought to church once or twice a year to practice the act of confession. Now, I don't think the Catholic Church imposed this, but I had a sense that I could not go directly to God. I didn't think I could pray out of the outpouring of my heart—not that I even considered doing such a thing. Instead I thought I needed to pray rote prayers containing words I knew but never quite understood. Prayer was rigid and rehearsed with no feeling or connection with the One to whom I prayed.

Almost every Sunday when I was young, I sat with my family in church, I knelt before God, and I sang His praises, yet I did not know Him at all. None of us really did. And for all that time spent in church, we gained nothing because ultimately we were not pursuing God—we were merely practicing religion, completely unaware of an alternative that far surpassed anything we could conceive. There is a significant difference between practicing religion and following Jesus—one that is exemplified over and over in the Gospels. Jesus Himself rejected religion as He continually rebuked the Pharisees and Sadducees— the religious people of His day. So in my rebellion, when I thought I was walking away from God, what I was really rejecting—what I was really leaving behind—was religion. I saw religion as a hoax. All the hypocrisy. The ritual. The legalism. The lack of grace. It all seemed like such a lie.

And it turns out it was.

My rebellion against my parents had subsided by the time I got to college. My dad and I were close again, and my parents had even rekindled their friendship by that time as well.

I studied history and writing at the University of Nevada, Reno, which only intensified my rejection of religion. As I learned about the history of "the Church," I was so convinced that the whole Christianity thing was a modern-day myth that I shelved the Bible that I was made to purchase for a humanities course next to all my other books about Greek and Roman mythology. I found it interesting that an organization with such a sordid history could claim to be an agent of truth. Church history is littered with corruption and hypocrisy—the use of indulgences, efforts to keep commoners illiterate to retain control over the masses, the elaborate lifestyle of the clergy, and offering pilgrimages as a source of penance—all of which seemed to prove the illegitimacy of the Church. God and the Church and religion were all synonymous to me—inseparable. Never once did it occur to me that I might be able to have God apart from, what I considered, corrupt institutionalized religion, and so I rejected God along with the Church.

I was never able to say with absolute certainty that God is not real, but I highly doubted His existence. The truth of God's existence, in my mind, was ultimately unattainable. I didn't think anyone could know whether God exists, nor did I think anyone could accurately assess the divinity of Jesus. I wasn't opposed to having faith but, quite simply, I didn't see any proof. And I certainly wasn't going to be one of those "blind faith" suckers.

In the absence of God, I was the highest authority in my life. I was the one in control. I was the one who defined what was right or wrong, based on my own sovereign moral compass. And with that, I had functionally become my own god. I had effectively bowed down to worship the god of self.

It was all about control. I liked having control. I thought I had control over my life, but I didn't. Control is merely an illusion. That fact became painfully apparent to me years later when I fell into anxiety and depression. After that, there was no fooling myself into thinking I had control, and that scared me. I was completely out of control, and I did not yet know the One who held all things together.

So when I walked through those church doors with Travis and the girls for the first time in many years, fear filled my heart. For some reason, I was completely terrified. But even greater than my fear was my desperation. My last shred of hope was that God could help me. I was so surrounded by darkness—around and within—that I wondered if others could actually see it. I was a complete mess, and there was absolutely nothing I could do about it. I had no more answers. All my options had been exhausted. And I could not save myself this time.

I never thought it was possible for God to show Himself, but I was wrong. As I listened to the pastor preach, I was entirely astounded and surprised to hear a sermon that seemed to have been written just for me. The message spoke to where I was that exact moment, and it blew my mind. It was powerful, beyond anything I had ever experienced, and I thought, *The sheer probability of that alone is crazy!*

Travis and I met Pastor Dan after the service. He gave us a mug filled with goodies and a pamphlet introducing newcomers to Grace. I read the pamphlet as I lay in bed that night next to Travis. Most of it seemed innocuous enough, but I was a bit startled when I read their belief statement. One by one, I read the list—thinking, *these people are crazy!*—while fear and defeat gripped me by the throat. *What if this is simply yet another rabbit trail, like all the others,* I wondered. *What if I never get better?* In all my searching, all my pursuits to get better, I continually came up empty-handed. And, in that moment, it seemed this pursuit would be just like all the others. It was yet another mirage promising life that would soon reveal itself to be a lie.

"Can you read this?" I said to Travis, passing the pamphlet to him.

He read through the pamphlet as I stared at him, anxiously waiting for him to reel back in disbelief as I had. But when he finished, he simply handed it back to me and said, "It's good."

It's good? At the very least, I expected Travis to call some of these crazy beliefs into question, but he didn't. He didn't question their belief in the validity of the Bible—that it's completely inspired by God and free of all error. He didn't dispute the claim that there is only one way to heaven, through the blood of Jesus, though it seemed ludicrous to believe the blood of some guy who lived thousands of years ago could "save" us. Nor did he balk at the one belief that really had my head spinning—the claim that all other world religions are false, a result of Satan's deception.

"So you believe this stuff?" I asked.

"Yeah. There's nothing weird in there."

I set the pamphlet down on my nightstand and pondered anxiously a few moments before picking it up again. I couldn't stop myself. I had to read it again. Perhaps I was mistaken. Perhaps there's a different way to look at it. Travis—noticing my irrational behavior and knowing me well enough to realize I was thinking entirely way too much—asked, "What are you doing?"

"I just don't know how these people can believe this stuff. I mean it's just—"

"Do you know what you need to do?" he interrupted.

"What?"

"You need to get up, take that pamphlet, throw it away, and go back to church next Sunday."

I was a bit stunned by Travis's response, but I complied.

We went back to church the following Sunday and every Sunday after that, each time fully expecting the God-thing to be a fluke. *How could a God so grand and so holy take notice of mere man?* I thought. But time and again, Jesus faithfully showed Himself.

It wasn't just in church, either. Strange things began to happen all the time, things I couldn't explain. One night, Ella—who was three at the time—called me into her room after I had put her to bed. She said, "Mommy, you know that Jesus loves you, right?" Tears stung my eyes as I stood in her doorway, startled by her comment. We didn't talk about Jesus at home. She knew very little about God herself, yet here she was, a little three-year-old, giving a message from God to her mommy.

Another time, Avery—who was one—began crying inconsolably after bedtime, which was not like her at all. By eleven o'clock, after spending hours trying to calm her down, I felt exhausted and defeated. Nothing I did worked. So as a last resort, I threw my hands up and said a prayer, fully convinced it wouldn't work. I didn't think God could really hear me and, even if He could, I certainly didn't think He'd pay much attention to my little problems. But I stood over my little girl and prayed anyway. I asked Jesus to calm her heart and give her peace so she could go to sleep. And that moment—and I mean that very moment— she fell asleep while I stood looking at her in amazement. Tears ran down my cheeks. *You are real*, I thought. *You do hear me.*

There are so many stories like these. It seemed God showed up daily. And I was given the proof I needed.

It was true; I couldn't save myself. So I was given grace. And as my eyes were opened, I began to see clearly for the first time. I began to see God's love. His mercy. His grace. His forgiveness. Yet I was still fighting. All along the way, I fought as I tried to apply reason to faith. But in the end, Jesus won—as He always does. He rocked my analytical world, tore down my every argument, turned my life upside down—or perhaps right side up—and gave me life.

The moment we surrender ourselves to Jesus, we're made new. We're made alive in Christ, and this is precisely how I felt. I felt free for the first time as I began to be healed of the anxiety and depression that had held me captive for months. The joy and peace I so desperately sought finally took residence in my heart. And the void that I had been unknowingly trying to fill with worldly things—accomplishments and accolades that ultimately led me down the dark alley of my soul—was filled with the light and love of Christ.

I had been made new.

Yet as I began to live out the Christian life, I soon realized this thing was going to be harder than I had originally thought. Many Christians try to win people over to Christ by painting fanciful pictures of what life will be like after coming to Jesus, giving the impression that all their problems, all their pain, and all their difficulties will disappear instantly upon praying the prayer of salvation. But this is simply not true. I don't believe these well-meaning Christians are deliberately trying to deceive anyone. Part of what they say is true. We do, after all, serve an amazing God who redeems. But this prosperity gospel is a farce. God is not some cosmic genie in the sky, granting our every wish, pacifying us to simply make us happy. Instead, the God of the Bible is the God who created us, knows us intimately, understands the "big picture" as we never can, and uses His sovereign knowledge and power to work all things—including our pain and our trials—according to His purpose for our good and His glory.

It seems to me that following Jesus is metaphorically less like skipping through a meadow, hand in hand with God, and more like summiting Mount Everest. Don't get me wrong: becoming a Christ follower is amazing—it's the greatest gift we can receive—but it's not always a stroll in the park. And when I was a baby Christian, following Jesus seemed to be a constant struggle—so much so, that I began to question whether something was wrong with me.

After a church service one day, I spoke with one of my pastors. "I feel like I'm on a roller coaster ride," I said. "It seems everything is fine and relatively calm for a little while, but then I plunge hard into this crazy whirlwind of trials. I come out of it momentarily only to fall back into the disorienting mess all over again. Is that normal?"

"It can be," he responded.

I was a new believer. And the battle was on. But I was a bit disillusioned because I thought that once I came to Christ, everything would settle down a bit. That my newfound faith would be a fix-all, of sorts. I knew my life wouldn't be perfect, but I did think it might get easier. I had this notion that God doesn't allow believers to go through the storms of life to the same extent that nonbelievers do, but this simply is not the case. I believe the battle intensifies once we come to Christ, for with Christ comes a new enemy: Satan.

Over time, as I matured in faith, the struggles decreased in frequency and intensity, but the battle remained. Following Jesus was hard, but I loved my new life. My life is far richer today than it ever was before Jesus. I echo Paul's words in Philippians 3:8, which reads: "Indeed, I count everything as loss because of the surpassing worth of knowing Christ Jesus my Lord. For his sake I have suffered the loss of all things and count them as rubbish, in order that I may gain Christ." Now, I can't claim loss as Paul did—and I refuse to play victim because I don't believe I am one—but just as Paul states, I believe nothing compares to knowing Jesus. Nothing comes even close. I'd rather lose everything I have than lose my Savior. Knowing Jesus is the greatest gift I have ever and will ever receive in this life.

In my darkness, Jesus beckoned, "Come to Me," and I came running with what little hope I had left. All I asked was to attain some semblance of normalcy again. I wanted my life back. I wanted my body and mind to work properly again, but what I received was something far greater than what I ever conceived. The moment I came to Christ, my entire life changed. I changed. I became a different person. Perspectives changed. Worldly "truths" shattered as I was transformed by God's truth. Life finally began to make sense. Purpose permeated my life, igniting my soul as it never had before.

It turns out life's purpose really isn't such a riddle, after all. It's much simpler than most people think, but it takes spiritual eyes to discern. The purpose of life is *God*. To know and be known by the One and Only. The One who loves immeasurably more than we imagine. The One who gave everything to reconcile us to Himself that we might have a relationship with Him. It's profound yet simple—beautiful. It is God who gives purpose. And it is God who is our purpose. Life is about loving God and loving others—magnifying Him so that the whole world may see and know that He is who He says He is. That He may take His rightful place in our lives, bringing joy to both God and the world. This is shalom, everything as it ought to be. He is the peace we so desperately seek.

Chapter 4

"FOLLOW ME"

They say time heals all wounds, but that's simply not true. Time only dulls the pain. God heals the wounds.

I had a fire in my belly like never before. As I sought Jesus with a heart full of passion and purpose, everything I knew to be true was questioned. Every worldly truth I had previously held was abandoned as the truths of the gospel took hold of my mind.

I was thirsty for truth—and for God. When I wasn't reading my Bible, I was listening to sermons on podcast while doing chores, soaking in the richness of God's Word. Reading the Bible was like reading a good book, the best book I had ever read—I couldn't put it down. And it changed me. The more I immersed myself in the Scriptures, the more I became someone I never thought I would be.

I had been a skeptic—a scoffer, even. But now all I wanted was to give everything to Jesus, to the God who plucked me out of darkness and brought light to my life. I began to pray: *Lord Jesus, let me live my life for You. I give it all to You. Empty me of myself, and use me for Your purposes, for Your glory.*

Yet I was still broken.

The anxiety hit hard when it first came. The once fearless, self-sufficient, social woman I knew crumbled, leaving in her place a scared little girl who had little energy to get out of bed each morning. Panic attacks came out of nowhere, with no warning, and fear quite literally paralyzed me. It was all so irrational, and the worst part was that I knew it was irrational, but I didn't know how to conquer it.

Within several months of giving my life to Jesus, however, God had already shown Himself mighty, bringing soundness to my mind once again. The depression had gone away completely. The anxiety—though it still reared its ugly head from time to time—was nothing like before, and it didn't scare me as much. God had plucked me up out of a ridiculously deep, dark pit, and I knew I could do anything with Him by my side.

For a while, it seemed that I was truly healed. But I would soon discover that I had a ways to go. It turned out I was going to need Jesus far more than I had originally thought.

It didn't take long to notice that my irritability had not gone away. I was irritable all the time and quick to anger and, let me tell you, it was not pretty. Travis and the girls took the brunt of it, and I hated myself for that. And to be honest, I was a bit perplexed as to why I struggled so much in this area. I didn't know why I was so grumpy all the time. Every time I lost my temper and snapped at my family, I felt instant condemnation and defeat. *Why can't I just be nice, Lord?* I'd pray. *What is wrong with me?*

As a child, I had always been the "nice" girl. I never wanted to cause any issues because I knew Mom had plenty to deal with already with my sister and all her medical challenges, so I resolved to be nice. I was the easy child—the one who gave Mom very little grief prior to my teen years.

But I couldn't be nice anymore. I couldn't control my feelings. It seemed I was completely at the mercy of my emotions, and I knew I could not fix myself. I had tried that and failed miserably. But I knew God could do it. He had done it before in other areas, and I was certain

He would do it again. So I began to pray, asking Jesus to show me why I was irritable, asking for healing once again. And then God showed me the root of my irritability. It was anger. That surprised me. You would think that wouldn't have come as a shock considering my past, but it did.

You see, I didn't *feel* angry all the time. I felt irritable. But at this point in my life, my anger wasn't a surface-level anger; it went much deeper than that. And as God shed more light on this issue, I came to understand that what I was really dealing with was not a touch of anger here and there—it was bitterness.

People who are bitter had always put a bad taste in my mouth, and I swore, in my pride, that I would never be like "those kind of people." But I had become one. It's humbling when God shows you you've become like the very people you don't like.

I suppose it was bound to happen, though. Anger unresolved turns to bitterness every time. But my anger was not unresolved by choice. I wanted to heal. In fact, I had tried to will myself into a place of healing for close to a decade. At the time of the murder, I did my best to allow myself to grieve, to feel my emotions. After that, I tried to stay positive and let time do its work. But despite my best efforts, I could not heal myself. No measure of time or positive thinking or choosing to forget my past would ever bring true healing. During the previous nine years, I had effectively and unintentionally buried my anger and my pain. But it doesn't take a genius to realize that unresolved feelings rise to the surface sooner or later.

Bitterness is ugly. I was ugly. And I didn't like myself very much at this point. I knew I needed healing. I was desperate for healing. But not the kind of healing the world offers. I didn't need to take an anger-management class. I didn't need additional counseling or additional time to heal my wounds. You see, the world can only offer you so much. I had tried every worldly solution with no real success. Worldly counsel—which promises so much and delivers virtually nothing—had proven to be of little help in my case. And I am absolutely certain this is true for every one of us, because healing—true healing—comes through God alone. What I needed was Jesus.

In my prayer journal, I wrote:

Heal me completely, Lord! Help me to heal emotionally—I give my anger and bitterness to You. Resolve them! Soften my heart. Tear down my walls! Break through to me and save me. Take away the burden of being the "girl whose dad was murdered." Take away my grief, my fear, my anxiety, my distrust, my bitterness, my anger, and replace it all with trust in You and knowledge of who I am in You. . . .

Heal me, Lord! I give myself to You completely to do as You will— tell me what to do, and I'll do it!

Soon after, I heard God's gentle whisper—*It's time to forgive.*

I knew what God was calling me to. I knew whom I was being called to forgive, but I thought I had already done that. I rarely thought about Anthony, and when I did, I didn't feel hatred or anything like that. Yet over the course of the next several weeks, God slowly showed me that, while I had forgiven Anthony as far as I was capable, I needed *His* grace to forgive completely, to forgive unconditionally.

But then God took it a step further.

While the girls were napping one day, I picked up Billy Graham's book *The Journey.* I had been reading this book for some time and really enjoyed gleaning wisdom from such an influential man of God, but I certainly wasn't ready for what God was about to say to me through Dr. Graham's words that day. I read:

Pray not only for your friends but for your enemies. Elsewhere in the Sermon on the Mount Jesus declared, "You have heard that it was said, 'Love your neighbor and hate your enemy.' But I tell you: Love your enemies and pray for those who persecute you" (Matthew 5:43–44). As Jesus was dying on the cross, He looked at those who crucified Him and prayed, "Father, forgive them, for they do not know what they are doing" (Luke 23:34).

You cannot pray for someone and hate them at the same time. Even if you are asking God to restrain their evil actions, you should also be praying that He will change their hearts. Only eternity will reveal the impact of our prayers on others. Prayer is one way we put the Golden rule into action.*

Love your enemies.

Really? I thought. *I need to love my enemy?* I knew what God was telling me, but I was not happy about it. Some truths are so much easier to swallow in concept than in reality. It's one thing to read God's commands, nodding in agreement from the comfort of a chair. And it's quite another to be asked to actually live out these commands. To actually do them.

I cried out to God and said, "Okay, God, I get the whole forgiveness thing, but love my enemy? How am I to do *that?*"

Immediately, His response came, "Bring him a Bible."

I have only heard from God like this a few times. I'm certainly not one who claims God speaks audibly to me, though I'd love it if He did. This was more like a thought planted into my mind immediately following my prayer, and I knew it was a word from God. In fact, it was a definitive command.

Questions filled my mind as I sat in silence. *Bring him a Bible?* I prayed. *What good would that do, Lord?* Anthony claimed to be a Christian at the time of the murder—which I had chalked up as yet another rebuttal against Christianity, another reason I had rallied against religion for so long. I was sure Anthony already had his own Bible, so it didn't make sense. But I knew what I had heard.

---

*Billy Graham, *The Journey: How to Live by Faith in an Uncertain World* (Nashville: Thomas Nelson, 2006), 212.

I grabbed my Bible off my nightstand and pored over the Scriptures, looking up every verse pertaining to forgiveness and loving my enemy. I read each one. I copied them down. I prayed. And then I simply sat there. Completely still.

I knew what I was being called to do.

The question was, would I obey?

One of my favorite phrases in the Bible is "but God." I have it posted beside my bed, and every so often my girls ask me why I have those two little words there. I tell them, "All through the Bible bad things happen—people sin or something goes wrong—but over and over two words make it all okay: 'but God.'"

You see, no matter what happens in life, no matter how bad things seem to be, God is still the constant. He is still working all things for good. The psalmist wrote, "My flesh and my heart may fail, *but God* is the strength of my heart and my portion forever" (Ps. 73:26, emphasis mine). Joseph echoed this sentiment when he said, "As for you, you meant evil against me, *but God* meant it for good" (Gen. 50:20, emphasis mine). Yet in my mind, the ultimate "but God" statement in the Bible is, "*But God* shows his love for us in that while we were still sinners, Christ died for us" (Rom. 5:8, emphasis mine).

Jesus truly is our Redeemer. Seeing Him as such allows us the freedom to trust and surrender ourselves to Him. We need to know our God. We need to know who He is and what He has done. It is only then that we are able to understand that He is for us, not against us, which frees us to obey, knowing He will work all things for our good and His glory.

Coming to understand God's heart toward me—that He loves me, that He is for me, and that He is my comforter and my guide—suddenly empowered me to live life differently. Sure, I was a newbie at this whole Christian thing, but I knew I served a faithful, loving God.

I knew I could trust Jesus, for He had proven Himself trustworthy. That didn't mean God's call to love and forgive Anthony was easy to embrace. I was scared. I didn't know where this was going. And I certainly didn't know how it would end. But I also knew I had allowed fear to motivate me far too long.

Fear is a God-given emotion. Its purpose is to protect us from harm. This kind of fear is good. But so much of the fear we experience is irrational fear—fear that holds us back from living the full life Jesus died for us to have, fear that holds us hostage, never allowing us to see true growth of character. This kind of fear never brings good. And if we choose to live in irrational fear, we will never see the promises of God fulfilled to the extent they're given. We will never follow Christ into our hard places and come out greater on the other side.

Here's the truth. Sometimes, we simply need to do it scared. Over and over at this time, well-meaning Christians told me to "follow peace." I wasn't to move forward if I didn't feel peace about taking a step. But the whole "follow peace" thing can be a ploy—shrouded in holy words—used by Satan to bind us and keep us from following God. Jesus calls us out of our comfort zones into places of discomfort. And in these areas, we're not going to feel peaceful all the time. Yes, there is the peace of God that surpasses all understanding and is available to believers at all times, but often our propensity to rely on ourselves and do things our own way hinders us from experiencing that peace, which means sometimes following Jesus feels a bit crazy. A bit unsettling. Oftentimes we will feel scared to do that which God calls us to do. But make no mistake—fear does not negate the call. Fear is simply a by-product of our desire to control. When following Jesus into our unknown, scary places, God doesn't usually clue us in on the big plan. And this can feel anything but peaceful at times. But still, we must move.

In my prayer journal at the time, I wrote, "I am seeing more and more that the Christian life is *not* a life of passivity, but a life of choices empowered by the Holy Spirit. I pray, Lord God, for You to help me to walk in Your Spirit."

I heard it once said we can choose to live each day motivated by fear or by faith. It's a choice we must all make. Christian reformer Martin Luther wrote in the preface to his translation of the epistle to the Romans, "Faith is a living, unshakeable confidence in God's grace; it is so certain, that someone would die a thousand times for it."* I needed this kind of faith. I needed *great* faith to move beyond my fear and follow Jesus where He was leading. I needed the kind of faith that allows us to step out of the boat and walk on water toward Jesus when He beckons, knowing that we can do all things through Him. The kind of faith that confidently says to Jesus, "Only say a word, and I shall be healed," knowing full well that all things are possible with God. The kind of faith to follow Jesus into the unknown—into my scary places—regardless of the cost, knowing He will work all things for good.

I spent most of the night in prayer, asking Jesus for grace. I desperately needed His grace to trust and follow Him where He was leading. I prayed for Him to grow my faith. To allow me to see as I ought.

And as Dr. Graham's words came to mind once again—about how Jesus loved and prayed for His enemies, even as He hung on that cross—I thought, *what is Jesus really asking me to do, anyway?* Then it hit me. He was simply asking me to give that which I had already received. That night, I began to see and understand the gospel more fully. I began to see that, prior to coming to faith in Jesus, I was in fact an enemy of God. Yet while I was still far from God, He loved me, He pursued me, and He died for me—even in my rebellion.

God loves His enemies.

I understood more deeply that Jesus's death brought me life. Life I did not deserve. Jesus died so we could be forgiven and reconciled to the Father. He died to atone or to pay for our sins. You see, Jesus's death

---

*This translation was made by Bro. Andrew Thornton, OSB, for the Saint Anselm College Humanities Program. ©1983 by Saint Anselm Abbey, Manchester, NH.

was necessary. There was no other way. We are sinners, and the penalty of sin is death—or eternal separation from God—but God couldn't let that happen. His love for us demanded that He do something to bring us back to Himself, to the only place we will ever find true life. The only place we will ever be whole. So it was Jesus who, in our place, paid the cost for our sins. And it was Jesus, God incarnate, who loved His enemies unto death that He might call us *friend*.

Jesus's death made forgiveness possible. I have been forgiven, just as each and every follower of Christ has been. Scripture tells us that we "were bought with a price" (1 Cor. 7:23). *Who am I to withhold forgiveness and love from my enemy,* I thought, *when it has been so graciously given to me?* I think C. S. Lewis said it well: "To be a Christian means to forgive the inexcusable because God has forgiven the inexcusable in you."*

I look to Jesus dying on the cross, hands and feet pierced only moments before, saying, "Father, forgive them, for they know not what they do" (Luke 23:34), and I continue to be amazed by His ability to forgive those who were *in the process* of murdering Him. It is this example we must follow. This is our motivation to forgive. And as Christ followers, we're given the power to forgive as Christ does, through the Holy Spirit.

But ultimately, forgiveness is not an option. It's a command.

That may seem harsh, but it's certainly not intended to be. Any command given by God is ultimately motivated by love. God is not just loving but, as the Bible says, God *is* love (1 John 4:8). That's who He is. It's part of His character. He is the complete embodiment of love. And with that in mind, we can infer that any command He gives or any action He takes comes from a place of love—regardless of whether it appears to be so. God knows what is best for us, and this command to forgive is for our good and His glory.

---

*C. S. Lewis, *The Weight of Glory: And Other Addresses* (New York: Harper Collins e-books, 1980; originally published 1949), 238.

As these truths swirled around in my mind, I was given grace to follow Jesus and embark on a journey toward forgiveness and healing. I wouldn't be able to forgive on my own. I knew that much. So I needed to lay down my pride and allow God to give me strength and grace enough to forgive. It was His work that needed to be done. I simply needed to obey.

Now, I understood my need to forgive, and I knew forgiving Anthony would bring me to a better place. I wanted to forgive. The thing that I did not want to do was love my enemy. The word *love* in the same sentence as *enemy* didn't seem to make sense to me. What's more, the word *love* in reference to Anthony was repulsive.

But this is what the Bible tells us to do. Jesus says, "Love your enemies and pray for those who persecute you" (Matt. 5:44). I didn't quite understand it. I wasn't sure what prayer would do. But according to this verse, I needed to pray. So out of obedience, I began to pray for Anthony. I prayed good things for him, though it was counterintuitive to all that was inside me. While I did not hate Anthony at this point, as I once did, a lot of negative feelings were still associated with him. Even saying his name felt vile. But I prayed nonetheless. I prayed that God would change him. I prayed that God would heal him. I prayed that God would bring him to complete repentance. And I even prayed that Anthony would be transformed by the gospel to the extent that he would be motivated to live to the glory of God in prison, bringing many prisoners to know and serve Jesus.

It felt wrong, praying for Anthony—as if I was betraying my dad. But I knew the ways of God are always right, regardless of how we feel.

A lot had happened since reading about loving my enemy that night. The next morning, I contacted the prison and was told I needed to be put on a visitors list in order to see Anthony. They said both Anthony and the warden would have to approve my visit, a process that could take months.

That's not what I wanted to hear.

Months is a long time. I wanted to get it over with. My thought process went something like this: *God told me to do something. I want to obey and be done with it. Quickly.* I thought it would be relatively easy to obtain the visitation approval. After all, God was calling me to this. Surely He would open all the right doors and allow me to see Anthony in a timely fashion; and once all the doors stood open before me, I'd be able to walk into that prison and say whatever God intended for me to say. I would tell Anthony I forgave him and, voilà, I'd be healed. It was a good plan, I thought. But oftentimes God's plans differ from ours, and it turned out, I needed to be patient.

So I prepared to wait.

Not knowing if Anthony would be receptive to see me, I decided to write him a letter, asking him to approve my visit, reassuring him that I intended no harm. While writing, I thought of Romans 12:17–21:

> Repay no one evil for evil, but give thought to do what is honorable in the sight of all. If possible, so far as it depends on you, live peaceably with all. Beloved, never avenge yourselves, but leave it to the wrath of God, for it is written, "Vengeance is mine, I will repay, says the Lord." To the contrary, "if your enemy is hungry, feed him; if he is thirsty, give him something to drink; for by so doing you will heap burning coals on his head." Do not be overcome by evil, but overcome evil with good.

"Overcome evil with good."

As I thought about how to apply this Scripture, I realized every person—regardless of who they are or what they've done—deserves to be treated with dignity and kindness. If I were to have any impact on Anthony for good, I would have to live out this Scripture. As I wrote the letter with God's truth in mind, I chose kindness above feelings and began to understand a bit more about how to love my enemy. After finishing the letter to Anthony, I wrote a friend, saying, "At this point, I have done what I can do. It's up to God to open the doors further."

But I was still scared. I was initiating contact with a murderer—one who had already spent close to a decade in prison. *Perhaps he's gotten really good at conning people*, I thought. *What if he deceives me?* Fear bubbled up, telling me lies, trying to convince me to abort my journey when it had only just begun. But then Jesus pointed me to Psalm 23 (emphasis mine):

The LORD is my shepherd; I shall not want.
>   He makes me lie down in green pastures.
He *leads me* beside still waters.
>   He *restores* my soul.
He *leads me* in paths of righteousness
>   for his name's sake.

Even though I walk through the valley of the shadow of death,
>   *I will fear no evil,*
for you are with me;
>   your rod and your staff,
>   they comfort me.

You prepare a table before me
>   *in the presence of my enemies;*
you anoint my head with oil;
>   my cup overflows.
Surely goodness and mercy shall follow me
>   *all the days of my life,*
and I shall dwell in the house of the LORD
>   *forever.*

Amen, I wrote in my Bible at the end of the passage. I closed my eyes, silently giving thanks to God for His timely encouragement, and felt my fear dissipate. I knew I would be okay.

As I thought about the possible visit, I tried to envision Anthony in his prison cell. I thought about sitting across from this man—the man who murdered my dad—and what that might be like. I didn't know why God was calling me to see him. And I didn't know what I'd say. I certainly had a lot of questions. Loads of questions, really, that only Anthony could answer. But I still didn't know what to say, and part of me didn't want to know. I didn't want this to be from me. I didn't want to drive this train. I wanted God to. What I wanted was to follow God's lead and place my trust completely in Him, believing that if this really was where God was leading me, then He would be with me. God would give me the words.

A few days later, I wrote to a friend:

Frankly, I have no idea to what purpose God would send me there to see him. . . . All I know is that God seems to be leading me in this way, and I feel like I need to follow Him.

Crazy? Yes! But sometimes God calls us to do certain things that don't seem to add up at the time. Truly, what would giving Anthony a Bible accomplish? I don't know. Only God does! Perhaps it will be the pivotal point in Anthony's life that leads him to be completely transformed by the gospel and repentant. Maybe not, maybe it's God testing me and teaching me how to fully trust Him without using my logic (which is my problem). Maybe it's what I need for God to fully heal me from my past.

I was beginning a new journey. A journey toward forgiveness and healing. And though I didn't know where God would take me, or what I would encounter along the way, I knew God knew. And that was good enough for me.

Chapter 5

THE LETTER

This was not the first time I had thought about visiting Anthony. In the early years after the murder, part of me wanted to go into that prison just to make sure Anthony felt absolutely terrible about what he had done. I wanted to ensure he knew well the wake of destruction he had left behind. I wanted to yell at him. To tell him all the ways he had ruined his own life, my life, and the lives of those closest to me. I wanted to hurt Anthony—just as he had hurt me.

They say hurting people hurt people. I believe this to be true.

But why do people secretly revel at the thought of their enemy's misery?

Why do we have this detestable desire to know that our enemy feels pain?

Disillusioned, we often believe causing pain will somehow ease our own. We feel some sort of retribution must be paid for what our enemy did, and who better to enact that justice than ourselves, right? But justice is not ours for the taking, and inflicting pain on our enemy will not heal our own.

Inflicting pain never heals pain.

We cannot overcome evil with evil but must overcome evil with *good* (Rom. 12:21). Hate simply gives birth to more hate, and committing evil will only result in the presence of even more evil. Martin Luther

King Jr. once said, "Darkness cannot drive out darkness; only light can do that. Hate cannot drive out hate; only love can do that."* And he was right. I love this quote and believe it to be true with my whole heart because, you see, Jesus gives us a better way than the ways of this world. A way that is just and good. A way that allows good to prevail.

For all the years I wanted vengeance, I stood in the place of God. I hijacked the role of God, deeming myself judge and jury, when that role was never mine to hold. I knew it was about time I stepped down from that judgment seat and allowed God to take His rightful place on it. It was time I left Anthony to God's judgment. Because, after all, God alone is judge.

God had been at work in my soul. And He was working quickly. The girl who had been motivated by anger and vengeance, who wanted to go into that prison to inflict further pain and suffering, was now replaced with a woman whose sole desire was to follow God and bring good. No longer motivated by anger, no longer driven by emotions or pain, I pursued this visit for the purpose of bringing healing, not pain—with forgiveness and love as my means.

"Daddy!" the girls and I shouted in unison as Travis walked in the door from work one night. The girls leapt from their seats and ran into their daddy's arms as I stood making dinner, watching. Smiling.

Travis made the rounds, hugging and kissing each of us in the kitchen before setting a pile of mail down on the counter. He grabbed the letter on top and handed it to me. "You've got a letter," he said. I could tell it was no ordinary letter—Travis's expression made that clear.

"Thanks."

My heart quickened as I read the words "Northern Nevada Correc-

---

*Martin Luther King Jr., "Loving Your Enemies" (speech, Dexter Avenue Baptist Church, Montgomery, AL, November 17, 1957).

tional Center" stamped boldly on the back side of the envelope. It was from Anthony. A letter from Anthony.

Tears stung my eyes as I looked at Travis and spoke in a faint whisper, "I gotta . . . I gotta go," I said. "Take care of the girls."

Travis nodded.

I ran upstairs and into our bedroom, closing and locking the door behind me. As I sat on our bed, I placed the letter before me, not wanting to touch it. I stared in disbelief. *What do I do, Lord?* I prayed. *Help me, God. I need You—I can't do this without You.*

After some time, grace was given and my courage had built enough to pick up the letter and open it. It read:

Dear Laurie,

If you feel led to visit me I'm OK with that. If the prison has a special format for a one time visit, I'll sign the form. If not, and you have to get on a visitors list, let me know and I'll submit the paperwork. Please know that no matter what happens I am truly sorry for what I did, most especially to your family. I wish I could take back that day, every day. Again, Let me know what needs to be done and I'll do it.

Sincerely,

Anthony

"Most especially to my family"? *Does "my family" include my dad?* I thought. *Are you sorry for what you did to him or sorry for how the murder affected the rest of his family? Or perhaps you wish you "could take back that day" because you simply don't like paying the consequences of your decision.* Anger rose once again, and all the fluff surrounding the *idea* of forgiveness dissipated as I stood challenged by its reality.

There I was, holding a letter from *him.* I was holding paper *he* had touched. I was seeing *his* handwriting. These were *his* thoughts written on this paper I held. The same hand that pulled the trigger—not once but twice, killing my dad—had wielded the pen that wrote this letter.

My stomach churned.

I knew Jesus was calling me to love my enemy. To forgive. But this is *not* what I signed up for. This is *not* how I thought it would go. I wanted to visit Anthony—to talk to him, give him a Bible, and be done with it—not correspond with him. Never once did it occur to me that Anthony might respond to my letter. In my mind, the letter I sent to Anthony was strictly business, a means to an end that hopefully would result in his approval of my visit. A visit, mind you, that wouldn't take place for months.

This was *not* my plan.

I didn't want this letter. It brought me back to the darkest chapter of my life, and I really didn't want to go there. But I needed to. I knew I needed to. I knew Jesus was leading me toward forgiveness and healing, and, even though my path had taken an unexpected turn, I was determined to follow. No matter the cost.

I sat on the bed, reading the lines over and over—picking the letter apart, analyzing every word, every phrase—when I was struck with a thought. *My truth may not be God's truth.* And at that, I thought perhaps it would be beneficial to try to see this tragedy from a different point of view. I am the murder victim's daughter, after all, a position that lends itself to many biases. And as I recognized this, I began to ask myself very difficult questions.

What lies am I believing?

What biases have I taken into this situation?

How has my role as the "murder victim's daughter" colored the way I view this tragedy?

It was a pivotal moment. And in that moment, I began to pray: *Lord, let me see as You see. Let me see with fresh eyes. Let me shed my biases and no longer see this situation as the murder victim's daughter, but as You see—through the lens of the gospel.*

For the first time, God allowed me to see that my truth was not *the* truth. That my perceptions were, in fact, amiss.

I walked to my closet and took an old box off the top shelf. I had filled this box only weeks after Dad's death and had kept it ever since. It's my "Dad box," containing many cherished things of little use and little value that I hold on to simply because each of these items reminds me of my dad.

I set the box on our bed and opened the lid. A blue binder sat on top. I knew it was time to go through its contents, time to revisit my past. I needed to see with new eyes—eyes that had been opened to the truths of God.

As I pulled out the binder, I prayed for strength and began to read. Dad's death certificate, letters of condolence and support, every newspaper article printed covering the murder, notes taken during the trial, the Victim Impact Statement I gave during the trial, and much more lay within—compiled throughout the years to share with my children and nieces and nephews when grown. I read them all, praying, *Lord, let me see as You see.*

Hours passed. The girls were in bed, having peeked in when Travis let them in the room at one point to say good night. Finally, I finished. A sea of tissue—crumpled and used—littered the floor around me, as I whispered a prayer of thanks. God was working. I felt it. Old scabs tore off, revealing fresh wounds once again. But I was thankful, even though my heart bled.

"Tonight," I wrote in my prayer journal, "I've been reliving the trial and newspaper coverage—all of it. I desperately need Your wisdom. I recognize that my knowledge and wisdom are flawed, so I seek Yours. Please, Lord Jesus, guide me and show me what I should see."

The next morning, I called Pastor Bobby, the counseling pastor at my church. I desperately needed some good, godly counsel—counsel I knew Bobby could provide. I didn't want to go into this alone. I needed wisdom. And I certainly didn't want to assume that I had all the answers because I didn't—and I still don't.

I began rambling practically the moment Bobby said hello. Bobby must have thought I was a bit crazy. I didn't know him very well at this time, and there I was, calling out of nowhere, telling him about Dad's murder. I tried to fill him in on all God had done in my life in few words and little time, telling him I got a letter from the man who murdered my dad. Then I pretty much wrapped up by asking, "What do I do?" I think that's enough to make any pastor pause for a moment and think, "Wow. Okay then . . . Where to start?"

Bobby was amazing, though. He handled my ramblings well.

The thing was, I knew what God was calling me to do. I knew I needed God to enable me to forgive and love my enemy, but I didn't know what my role would be. How much of this would be God? And how much would require action on my part? Where does God stop and I begin? Or is it more fluid than that? Perhaps we work simultaneously. Together.

I had tried to will myself into a place of forgiveness for years, so I knew I couldn't do this on my own. But how do you forgive *with* God? And what is biblical forgiveness, anyway? Did what I believe about forgiveness line up with Scripture? Or did I have worldly misconceptions about forgiveness still swirling around in that head of mine? I had so many questions, but at the root of all these questions—what I was really getting at, what I really wanted to know—was if I was headed in the right direction.

Bobby confirmed my actions and said my theology seemed to be sound, much to my relief. I respect Bobby. His theology is good, and it was comforting to know I wasn't becoming some rogue fundamentalist—deceived both in mind and spirit—believing I was doing the will of God while actually practicing folly. After all, several people in my life strongly disagreed with what I was doing. But Bobby reassured me that I was headed in the right direction.

He told me that forgiveness is, in fact, a decision. That just as I had thought, faith is not intended to be something we simply have. The Christian life is not intended to be passive; our faith is supposed to be alive and active. We're to pursue and obey the commands of God.

Yet Bobby also pointed out that forgiveness is a decision that must be empowered by the Holy Spirit, as is every other part of our lives. For apart from God's involvement, this decision would lead nowhere. Without the empowerment of the Spirit, this pursuit of mine would end right where it had begun—and I'd be no better for it in the end, which I knew all too well.

During our conversation, I told Bobby about one of my main concerns. I feared that telling Anthony I forgave him would only lead him to think what he did was okay. But it wasn't. It would never be okay. I asked Bobby, "If I tell Anthony I forgive him, won't that justify his behavior in his own mind?"

"Laurie, Anthony is in prison," Bobby said. "He relives his mistake every moment of every day. Forgiving Anthony is in no way going to make him feel like murdering your dad was okay or justified because it wasn't, and he will be paying for what he did for the rest of his life. What forgiving him will do, however, is show him what the gospel looks like—what the gospel looks like in action."

I liked that.

"Okay," I said. "But then how do I love Anthony? Jesus is telling me to love my enemy, but how do I do that? Practically, I mean. What do I actually do?"

"You just keep doing what you're doing," Bobby said. "You are loving your enemy, Laurie. Keep doing that."

"Okay."

I can do that, I thought.

That night, in my prayer journal, I wrote:

Thank You, my Lord, my God, for this trial. Thank You for pointing me toward forgiveness. . . . I know it is Your will for me to forgive. . . .

Direct me! Make my path straight! I lift my soul to You and entrust myself to You! I know You will guide me and protect me but help me when I doubt!

Help me love my enemy. Show me what to do—do it through me! Bring Your light into my heart and let Your light banish all darkness within my soul!

I choose to forgive Anthony. I choose to love others, including my enemies! Help me to be Christ centered—other centered—at all times. Don't allow me to become self-absorbed during this process of forgiveness! Help me to deal with it in Your strength without becoming self-destructive and without losing sight of Your will! Thank You, my Lord! Thank You!

Anthony had agreed to see me. And I was one step closer. To what, I did not know. But after receiving Anthony's letter, there was no turning back. God had called me on this journey—I was certain of that—and if I were to see any victory in my life, I had to conquer this mountain that loomed large before me. Clearly, the only direction to go was forward. And so I would. One prayer at a time.

Chapter 6

SEEKING TRUTH

Everything was beginning to change. Call it a shift in perspective, if you'd like, but I believe it was more than that. I believe God was giving me new eyes to see what I had been missing all along.

*Should I call Diane?** I wondered. I really didn't want to call her, but I knew she had answers, and I needed her perspective.

Diane is the woman Dad was seeing at the time of his death—the one he seemed smitten with. But calling her with my questions would likely tear open some of her past wounds, and I certainly didn't want to do that. I didn't want to be the one to resurrect pain inflicted during the most heartbreaking years of her life. You see, Diane used to be married to Anthony. And as I'm sure you can conclude from that information, this relationship ultimately resulted in my dad's death. But it was complicated. Mistakes were made. Sins were committed. And the unthinkable was the result.

---

*Although Anthony's ex-wife testified at the trial and was identified by name in newspaper accounts of the murder and trial, I have changed her name throughout to protect her privacy.

After Dad died, Diane reached out to me quite a bit. She used to send little note cards to encourage me, saying that she hoped to be a blessing to me or that she was thinking of me. Every couple months or so, I'd find a little note of hers tucked into my pile of mail. While I appreciated Diane's notes, I don't think I ever did respond, and they eventually stopped coming. I think, in a way, that I was trying to cut ties with this part of my past and settle into my "new normal." It was nothing personal—I liked Diane. But I didn't want to establish a relationship with her. I think she reminded me too much of a part of Dad's life—and death—that I wanted to forget.

But I now had questions that needed answering. I wanted to know what Diane knew. I wanted to hear her side of the story. Even more than that—more than anything—I needed an answer to one specific question that had plagued me since the moment I was told of Dad's death. The question I sat pondering in the park that terrible afternoon after Dad's funeral: *Where has Dad gone? Is he in heaven?*

After coming to Christ, I began to understand the doctrine of salvation. Though confusion about life after death subsided, the question of Dad's salvation remained.

Was Dad saved? Did he know Jesus? I wondered.

I know only God can reveal this information, but I also knew that Dad and Diane had shared their faith with one another. Diane knew this part of Dad more than anyone. So I figured if anyone in this world could give me an indication of Dad's possible salvation, she could.

Clearly, it was time to call.

After putting the girls down for an afternoon nap, I made my way downstairs to my office. I sat at my desk and prayed for courage before dialing the number. As the phone rang, I nervously rehearsed what I wanted to say until I heard a woman answer on the other end.

"Hi. Is this Diane?" I asked.

"Yes, it is," the woman said.

I told Diane who I was, and we began to catch up. She was easy to talk to, and just as kindhearted as I had remembered. She asked about my life, and I told her all about getting married and having kids. I told her about my crazy emotional breakdown and how God had given me grace to believe. Diane brought me up to date on the happenings in her life over the last several years, and then I got to the point of the call.

"Can I ask you a question?" I asked.

"Sure, Laurie, anything."

"Well . . . when I went out to dinner with my dad, about a month or so before he died, he told me he had been going to church again. He started talking about Jesus, and, honestly, I think I dismissed much of what he was trying to tell me because it sounded like a bunch of nonsense at the time. But since coming to Christ, there's something that's really been bothering me. I know you and my dad spoke often. He told me you talked to one another about God. Honestly, I think you're the only one who would know, and I have to know—where was my dad in his faith when he died?" Tears stung my eyes as I willed my voice not to quaver. "Do you think he was saved?"

"Oh, Laurie, yes!" Diane said immediately. "I do believe your dad was saved. He was seeking—I mean really seeking. He went to his church every Sunday, and I went to mine. After, we would talk for what seemed like hours, telling each other all about the messages we had heard. Your dad had a lot of questions, and I tried to answer them. But yes, Laurie, I do believe he was saved." Diane paused. "You know, I have a letter your dad wrote to me. It's actually kind of like a written prayer that he gave me. Would you like me to read it to you?"

"Would you mind?" I asked, desperately wanting to know the content of the letter.

"Not at all. Let me go find it." Diane put the phone down as she found the letter Dad had written a decade before, and when she returned, she read one of the most beautiful things I have ever heard. Not because of the eloquence of Dad's words—he wasn't much of a word guy—but because it was a proclamation of his faith in Jesus. For close to ten years, I had felt plagued by the question of my dad's where-abouts, but now—upon hearing Dad's own words—hope began to rise. *Maybe Dad's heart was truly transformed and surrendered to Jesus prior to his death*, I thought. *Maybe, just maybe, Jesus plucked Dad up right out of that fire just in the nick of time.* If this were true, the implications would be astounding. It would mean that the very action that resulted in Dad's murder would also be the very thing that led to his salvation. The two would be inextricably linked. *Maybe this is what it took for Dad to come to Christ*, I thought.

Diane and I spoke a while longer. I was grateful that she was willing to go back to the time when her greatest wounds were inflicted in order to help me.

After we hung up, I dropped my head and closed my eyes, tears fall-ing like drops of rain from my lashes, and praised, *Thank You. Thank You, Lord.* I paused with my head down for a moment. When I looked up, my gaze involuntarily fixated on a picture of Dad and me that I framed and gave to him as a gift a few years before his death. It's one of my favorite pictures because it seems to capture the essence of our relationship. In it, Dad's giving me one of those crazy big bear hugs he often liked to give that practically crushed my rib cage—the ones I loved but hated all at the same time. The ones I now miss terribly.

When Dad died, the picture came to live with me and has sat upon my desk since that time. Yet in all the years it sat right in front of me, I never once saw the only thing that now captured all of my attention. There is a crucifix hanging on the wall beside Dad and me. And for whatever reason, I couldn't take my eyes off it. I sat—transfixed by what I had been missing all along, by what I believed God was now showing me—and God spoke. *He's okay*, He whispered. *He's Mine. Your dad is with Me.* A tidal wave of emotion swept over me. And I just knew.

Healing begins the moment we allow Jesus complete access to the darkness contained within our souls. Darkness flees in the presence of light, but light cannot go where it's not permitted. Doors must be opened for light's rays to touch our darkest dark. And I was flinging doors open left and right, begging, *Come, Lord Jesus, come.*

This is where it all begins, God whispered.

My healing had begun. The favor of God rested upon me—bringing peace through revelation about Dad's salvation—as I sought fervently to do His will. *Thank You, Lord. Thank You,* I praised in response. My dad had been saved within months, mind you, of his death. And as I caught my first glimpse of good's triumph over evil, I thought, *Surely, nothing is impossible for our God.*

Days passed, and the letter, still lying on my nightstand, beckoned a response. I didn't have one. How do you respond to the man who murdered your dad when he tells you, "I am truly sorry for what I did"? I realized Anthony's sentiments were better than what they could have been. "I'm sorry" is certainly better than defiantly expressing no remorse. But I wasn't convinced his apology was sincere, and the thought of possibly receiving a flippant "I'm sorry" from the man who took my dad's life was infuriating.

For days I thought about Anthony's apology and judged its sincerity, until God showed me one day that it was not my position to presume to know the condition of Anthony's heart. Where Anthony was emotionally and spiritually was beside the point. I was called to love and forgive my enemy, regardless.

I received the rebuke but still wondered how to do what God was calling me to do.

Day and night, I prayed for direction, for clarity, for eyes to see. And it wasn't long before I began to see my prayers answered.

I was beginning to change. Biases had polluted the way I viewed just about everything up to this point, but after recognizing my biases and choosing to approach this journey with fresh eyes and a softened heart, I began to see things differently.

Anthony's letter was my first interaction with him. Prior to this letter, we had never met. Admittedly, I knew very little about Anthony—and what I did know about him was derived from the few things Dad had told me before his death and what was said in newspaper coverage and court proceedings. Consequently, Anthony was more concept than reality in my mind. Though I knew he was a real person, he was—to me—more villain than man. He was, after all, the man who had murdered my dad, the man whose image sent chills up my spine each time I saw his mug shot in the newspaper. Anthony was the bad guy. The murderer. The one who, at the risk of sounding cliché, quite literally killed a part of my soul the day he murdered my dad. But as I held and read his letter time and again after its arrival, something happened.

Handwritten letters have largely been lost in our culture, but there's something to be said for taking the time to put pen to paper, for putting thoughts down by hand for another to read. Handwritten letters are personal, intimate—and now I had one from him. From my enemy. And though I didn't want it, there was something about this letter that had finally made Anthony real to me.

I began to see Anthony as a real person, just like me, with thoughts and feelings and life circumstances that molded and shaped him into the person he is. I began to question what happened in his life that allowed him to become the person who ultimately murdered my dad. What made him capable of killing another man? What was his childhood like? His family? What was his life like during the months and years prior to the murder? Was Dad's murder simply the culmination of a perfect storm, so to speak, or were there deeper things behind it? Pain, perhaps, from a childhood gone bad or some sort of mental illness?

As the days passed, I felt God's nudge to write back. But the thought of engaging this man in correspondence was unsettling. I was standing on rocky ground, and every step I took would undoubtedly lead deeper into enemy territory—deeper into the pain of my past. It was scary, but I knew this was where God was leading.

I needed to continue writing. I didn't want to, but it came down to logistics. I had already submitted my application to visit and felt I should tell Anthony that I hadn't pursued a one-time visit, as he had recommended, but that I had requested visitation rights altogether—rights Anthony would need to approve. So at this point, correspondence was simply a means to an end—the end being the visit I believed God was calling me to.

Nervously—but with confidence that I was following God's will—I sat at my computer and typed my second letter to Anthony, choosing each word with careful precision, letting kindness dictate my tone once again. As I wrote, I prayed that the love God was calling me to extend to Anthony wouldn't be mistaken for friendliness. I didn't want to give Anthony the wrong impression. I was doing this because God told me to—because I knew God was leading me somewhere significant—not because Anthony deserved it. Walking that fine line between kindness and friendliness, I thanked Anthony for his willingness to see me, told him I had already submitted my application, and ended by saying, "I'm not sure what this visit will accomplish, but this seems to be where God is leading."

Travis walked in the door from work a few weeks later with another letter in his hand. I wasn't sure if Anthony would write back this time, but he did. And though my response was much less dramatic, this new letter's presence was still unsettling. Standing in my kitchen, I held the envelope. With eyes shut, I took a deep breath and prayed, *Lord help me.* Then I opened the letter and read:

Dear Laurie,

I got your letter, if you already put in the paperwork at your end, you probably sped the process up. I've heard it can take 2 to 3 months though.

I don't know what it will accomplish either, but I'm glad you feel led by God to do it. If we leave it in His hands, only good can happen, even if it hurts.

Let me know when you get approved. We have visiting only on Friday and Saturday, and I play guitar on our church worship team and am in the chapel those days. So let me know what day, that way I can be outside.

If you feel led to write and ask me anything, I will always answer.

Also, I know your dad liked western stuff. I never did, but since that day I have tried to make it a part of my life. I'm not sure why except maybe to make sure I don't forget I took someone, and make it real to me. The music not so much, but I draw western pictures, if you would be interested in having one I'd be humbled.

Sincerely,

Anthony

P.S. I know you don't want me as a friend, and I'm not trying to "get you in my corner," so to speak. I just want you to know I'm a real person too, who regrets what he did and is just trying to do the best he can. Again, I'm so sorry.

I was confused.

Obviously, Anthony was involved with his church, but what did that mean? Was he really a follower of Christ? Had he changed, or was he truly a Christian at the time of the murder, as he had claimed? Is it even possible for a follower of Christ to commit murder?

Anthony offered to answer my questions, and I had many. But I wasn't sure whether I should ask them prior to the visit.

And what about the comment about western stuff? That seemed a bit odd. It was true—Dad was a cowboy at heart. He loved all things western. But why would Anthony want to draw a picture for me? And what would I do with a drawing from the man who murdered my dad? Frame it and hang it on my wall? That would be weird. Quite frankly, I didn't want it. I didn't want anything from Anthony—including these letters—but I was called to love my enemy. Something I was trying to figure out how to do. Was this what it looked like to love my enemy—to receive a gift from him?

Adding to the confusion, a friend directed my attention to Proverbs 28:17, which reads, "If one is burdened with the blood of another, he will be a fugitive until death; let no one help him." I wondered what that meant. I wondered how I was to love my enemy—an enemy, mind you, who happened to be a murderer—and ensure that the love I offered somehow didn't support him. Love by definition seems to support. Supporting Anthony was clearly not my intention, but giving kindness in love to someone could most assuredly be considered support. So how was I to reconcile my call with this Scripture?

I was at a loss.

Where do I go from here, Lord? I prayed. *Help me find Your will.*

I needed direction. I needed to feel Jesus tangibly hold my hand and hear Him say, "This way, my child. This way." But I heard nothing.

After praying and reading my Bible, I spoke to Travis and my girl-friend Sarah at length before e-mailing Pastor Bobby. I wrote:

I'm struggling with determining God's will in this situation.

On one hand, there's Proverbs 28:17, which says, "If one is burdened with the blood of another, he will be a fugitive until death; let no one help him." But on the other hand we are to love our enemies. How does one reconcile this? What does this mean? What does loving your enemy look like? I do feel like God wants me to go visit Anthony and bring him a Bible, but aside from that everything else is murky. Does God want me to visit and cut off all other contact or does He want more from me? I have absolutely NO desire to establish a relationship with this guy (obviously), but I don't know where this is leading, and I guess that's bothering me.

I'm just trying to figure out where God wants me to take this. I truly don't know. Maybe I don't need to know—perhaps God simply wants me to just follow His lead. But right now, I feel like I don't know what He wants me to do. Do I write back to Anthony's letter? Do I accept one of his drawings? Do I ask him questions via mail before visiting him? Does God want me to ask questions to prepare me prior to visiting him?

Maybe I'm just supposed to wait. To wait for God to direct me more clearly. That's what I've been doing thus far, but at what point does that become simply not acting on where I believe God is leading me? Does any of this make sense?

Anyway, I know you don't have the answers to all my questions. I'm just trying to feel my way through. I want so desperately to know clearly what God would have me do, but I just feel like I'm in the dark. Any advice?

Peace escaped me as I pondered my next move, but, to my surprise, all the physical symptoms of anxiety did not return—another testament to God's grace. A friend reminded me of Psalm 46:10—"Be still, and know that I am God." I said the words slowly to myself over and over, as if by doing so I would somehow retain their meaning to a greater extent. *Know. That. I. Am. God*, I repeated, taking slow, deep breaths.

"Follow peace, Laurie," my friend continued. "Listen for His direction."

I'm trying, I thought, desperately attempting to lay hold of it. I knew it was there for my taking. God tells us to receive His peace, and I'm pretty sure He wouldn't tell us to receive something that isn't there for taking. But silently, I wondered how. How do you receive something as elusive as peace?

With the girls down for another nap, I retreated to my bedroom. *I am His*, I reminded myself, as I flopped down on the unmade bed.

"He's got me," I whispered aloud, sighing with my eyes shut. I lay listlessly for a few minutes before remembering something I'd heard about Joseph in the Bible—something about him forgiving his brothers—and I thought perhaps his story, which I had yet to read, might bring clarity.

I reached for my Bible as I sat up in bed. Turning to the end of Genesis, I read the account of this extraordinary man and was encouraged to know that God has given us a story that puts flesh on His commands to love and forgive our enemies.

Joseph, who was sold into slavery by his brothers, had experienced many hardships as a result of his brothers' betrayal. Over the course of two decades, he had been sold, traded, and lied about, which ultimately resulted in his imprisonment. But after Joseph went through countless trials, God used every detail of Joseph's life to bring him to the point where God was able to exalt Joseph and set him over the affairs of Pharaoh, king of Egypt. Everything that had happened to Joseph was setting him up for God's ultimate call on his life.

I loved that.

I loved how this story exemplifies the sovereignty of God so well. In this story, I saw the favor of God woven throughout the good and the bad. I saw Joseph's perseverance and trust in the Lord, despite the unknown circumstances he continually encountered during his trials. And I saw God work all of Joseph's mess for the good of not only Joseph but also the whole nation of Israel.

In the end, Joseph had been given the gift of perspective. He was given eyes to see God's sovereign hand throughout every one of his hardships. To see that God had been intimately involved through every detail of his life and to see that God had used all of his pain for good. When forgiving his brothers, Joseph held great perspective on his life and the circumstances he endured, telling his brothers, "As for you, you meant evil against me, but God meant it for good" (Gen. 50:20).

"God meant it for good."

As I read this story, I believed my story would soon echo that of Joseph's, and I believed in that moment that God would use it all. All my pain, all my loss would be used for good. Nothing would be wasted. God would use it all, just as He had with Joseph, to masterfully create beauty and blessing. Beauty for ashes.

With all the unknowns still in place, I received peace as I took my eyes off the uncertainty of my circumstances and fixed them on God.

I got up and walked downstairs to see if Bobby had responded to my e-mail. I hoped his response would shine light on how I should proceed. As I sat at my desk, waiting for my mail to load, I hummed a little tune and thought about just how far God had brought me. I couldn't help but smile.

The mail came up. I saw Bobby's response and began to read:

Faith.

Proverbs 28:17 is talking about a tormenting guilt not found in the cross. The cross forgives even murder, thus we are to forgive even a murderer. Not to mention that we are guilty of murder in our hearts (Matt. 5:21–22).

Loving your enemy looks like what you are already doing. You just need to walk in it. As far as the future, you have no control over it. Remember, one step at a time, take it slow but stay the course.

All the other stuff is up to you. Use your best judgment and pull the trigger either way—accept the art or not, write first or not, continue visits, etc.

You're not in the dark because you're a child of light, and I trust you, so does God, for He entrusts us with the most important message He ever gave men (2 Cor. 5:16–21).

"I am not in the dark," I said aloud after reading Bobby's e-mail. "I am a child of light." *I am a child of light.* Closing my eyes, I let Bobby's words wash over me, thankful for the reminder of who I am and the message entrusted not only to me but to every Christ follower. A message that has forgiveness and reconciliation at its center.

I pondered my next step. "Use your best judgment and pull the trigger either way," Bobby had written. I wondered if it were really that simple. Didn't I need to wait for a clear message from God to proceed? I thought about this for a while but then realized that it would be against

God's very nature to fool His people. God is good. He is not out to trick us. My fear of being presumptuous, it seemed, was ill founded. Presumption is moving forward without prayer. It's going about our lives intent upon our own will. But if we diligently seek God—if we seek after His will even if it means His will doesn't line up with our own—we will never be fooled.

I prayed and asked for wisdom.

A few days passed. I decided to respond to Anthony and ask him a few questions. As I thought about what to ask, I remembered sitting in the courtroom during the trial, hearing Anthony's defense attorney claim, "It was an accident," as my family and I listened in disgust. We all knew Anthony's story was bogus—judge and jury included. Dad was not killed by accident.

But because Anthony's defense was driven by this "accident" lie, no one knew what really happened to Dad. No one knew what his last moments were like. What words he last spoke. What the tone of the conversation was like with Anthony moments before his death. I've always wondered if he was scared, having a .22 rifle aimed at his head as he sat, hands clasped together, on his couch. Did he know he was going to die?

What really happened inside Dad's house the night of the murder? I wondered.

No one knew—except Anthony.

With all these thoughts swirling around in my head and with Anthony's last letter sitting beside my laptop on my desk, I began to write.

Dear Anthony,

Thank you for your letter. I will let you know when I get approved, so we can set up our visit. Again, thank you for your willingness to see me.

As far as your western picture goes, if you feel as though you'd like me to have one, you may send one. Frankly, I've struggled with whether or not to accept a picture from you, but if you feel led to give me one, perhaps that's God's will.

While it is true that I have no desire to befriend you, I can see that you are a "real person." With that in mind, I do have some questions. But first, I'd like to appeal to you as a Christian to be honest with me. I understand that you do have many reasons that you would want to twist the facts, but God does call us all to honesty, so I'd ask you to please be straight with me. Additionally, in answering my questions, I'd like to ask you to please lay any agenda you may have aside and please answer me from your heart.

As you know, I attended your trial every day, so I know what was said there. What I would like to ask you, though, is for your story. Much light was shed on this topic during the trial, but I'd like to have your perspective. How did this happen? Why did this happen? What led you to this point? What really went on in my dad's house on August 5th? What was the tone of your conversation? What was said (on my dad's part as well as yours)? What set you off? Did my dad say something before you shot him? What were my dad's last words? Also, were you truly a Christian at this time or were you just going through the motions? Where are you at now as far as your faith goes?

I'm not asking for you to justify what you did because what you did can never be justified, and it will never be okay. But I do realize that you have insight into the situation that I have yet to hear. As much detail as you can provide would be much appreciated.

Thank you for allowing me to ask you questions.

Sincerely,

Laurie Coombs

A few weeks later, Anthony responded and said:

Dear Laurie,

Wow, do you have any easy questions!

I think these are questions best answered when you visit, face to face. I think things can be misinterpreted in a letter. I know this because it has happened to me. But I will set aside my appeal, trust you, and be honest. I don't want to hurt you any more than I have, so please be sure of the things you want to know. Just let me know when you are cleared, and we will talk about it all.

Til then, take care, and do this for me; you and your husband treat each other, every day, as if it's the first day you fell in love because that's what stops these kinds of tragedies from happening.

Sincerely,

Anthony

Who the hell does he think he is? I thought. *"Do this for me"? What gives him the right to speak into my life? I mean, he's right about the whole marriage thing—it's sound advice—but what nerve to think he can give me any advice at all!*

Anthony's response was infuriating and, quite frankly, annoying.

He's hiding something, I thought. *Perhaps he doesn't want to go on record with the truth. Perhaps it could affect his appeal.* I knew his story was a lie, and this response seemed to confirm my suspicions.

Don't tell me I can ask you anything and then refuse to answer my questions, I thought. *"Do you have any easy questions!" What did you expect? You murdered my dad! There are no easy questions!*

I took a breath. *Calm down,* I told myself. *I will get my answers soon enough.*

Chapter 7

ROADBLOCKS

I knew an immediate response to Anthony would be anything but lov-ing. I really had nothing constructive to say, so I figured I should sim-ply ignore Anthony's last letter and settle in to wait for my visit to be approved. I put the letter in a binder with the others and tried to put the whole thing out of my mind.

Summer was quickly approaching. My family and I decided to take a trip to the Ruby Mountains, one of Dad's favorite places. The Rubys are located in the middle of rural Nevada, and though this part of my state isn't quite known for its beauty, the Rubys stand in contrast to their surroundings like a towering oasis of pure beauty in the midst of nothingness, encompassed by dry Nevada desert.

When I was a kid, my family and I went to these mountains to camp, fish, and hike, which was the plan for this trip as well. My brother and his wife at the time were coming down from Idaho, and the rest of us—including Mom and her husband, Gary; my sister and her kids; and Travis and the girls and I—would be coming from the Reno area. It was about a five-hour drive for us and somewhere around the same for my brother, which made it an ideal place to vacation together.

The drive felt long, but it somehow felt worth it as we dropped down into the valley bordering the mountains.

"Look girls," I said pointing to the towering range in the distance. "Those are the Ruby Mountains." I looked at Travis. We smiled.

We soon found ourselves ascending Lamoille Canyon toward our campsite, passing a sea of wildflowers and groves of quaking aspens, one after another. I thought of Dad and how much he loved these trees clothed in leaves that shimmer with each little breeze. It was June, late spring—arguably the most beautiful time in the Rubys.

I don't remember who got there first, but we all ended up together at one point or another and proceeded to set up camp while daylight remained. After dinner, we took a stroll by the river that runs through the campground, a river that holds many memories from my childhood. My brother and sister and I used to fish there with Dad each time we visited, as Mom watched from the rocky shore. We'd wade calf- or knee-deep into the icy water, poles high in the air, hearts filled with excitement as we cast our lines, anticipating a catch. To my recollection, we always seemed to catch fish at this river. They were usually little, nothing big, but to a child, every catch is magical. I think I squealed. I'm not sure if I actually squealed when I caught a fish, but it seems to me that I might have. Something in my memory tells me I did, but perhaps this squeal represents more of how I felt than what I did.

After fishing for a little while, I'd inevitably get bored and would take to dam building, either by myself or with one of my siblings. Like beavers, we'd spend hours constructing something that seemed like a fortress to us, but unlike beavers, we used river rock instead of debris. I remember watching the rushing water's route change as I stacked rock upon rock, hoping I'd be able to create my very own waterfall.

I love these memories, and I couldn't wait to give these moments to my girls. I think the dam building was probably my favorite memory of this river; so the next day, my girls and I plunged into that river along with Travis to build ourselves a dam. It was our turn to make with our children those memories that Dad and Mom had made with me, and the girls loved it.

Throughout our trip, it seemed I was reliving my memories. Hiking up the familiar mountain, I saw myself in my girls as they slowed our hike to make stop after stop to pick wildflowers, their little hearts drawn to God's beauty. I saw my girls with Travis, their daddy, and recognized myself with mine those many years ago doing what Dad loved best—hiking, picking wildflowers, and letting me ride on his shoulders when I tired.

Dad was in his element up there on that mountain—any mountain, really—and his joy was contagious. It seemed those times were so much simpler somehow. As a child on this mountain, I breathed the air of a carefree existence, one not tainted by pain, not jaded by loss.

But many years later, having experienced things I never thought possible, I was on a path seeking to love and forgive the man who robbed me of more moments like these. I felt I was on the right path, but part of me wondered if I was. I thought I was doing the right thing, but perhaps my actions weren't honoring to Dad.

As I hiked up that mountain, a mountain that holds so much of Dad, I took a deep breath, closed my eyes with my face to the sun, and prayed silently, *Lord, am I on the right path?*

To which I felt God whisper a resounding *yes*.

Soon after we got home, I stood in my kitchen, reading yet another letter. This one was not from Anthony. It was from his warden:

Dear Ms. Coombs:

Your visiting application was forwarded to this office for consideration. Due to safety and security concerns for the institution because you are the victim's daughter, we are not approving visiting privileges for you.

Sincerely,

John Peterson

That was it. Two sentences that seemingly brought this path to an end. "I've been denied," I told Travis as I held the warden's letter up.

Pots and pans brimmed with dinner, as the girls noisily chased one another around our kitchen island. I stood perplexed.

"Well," Travis said with concern in his eyes, "you can appeal."

"Yeah," I said, deep in thought.

Turning away, I seemed to retreat inward as I thought about what to do next. An appeal seemed to be my only option. But I wondered what I would say. How could I put the warden's mind at ease? How could I show him that I didn't pose a threat?

My heart felt heavy. I didn't understand why God would allow the warden to deny my application. Doesn't the Bible say that God will make our path straight? Shouldn't doors just fly open when God calls us to do something? Doesn't He level the ground we walk on, make the hills like chaff? I had faith, so why weren't my mountains moving?

When I set out to do this thing, I thought God would open all the necessary doors so I could walk straight into that prison and hand Anthony a Bible, but apparently God was not following my script.

I knew what I had heard—*Bring him a Bible.*

Forgive.

Love your enemy.

But how was I to do any of that if I couldn't visit? It didn't make sense.

I sat down to draft a letter to the warden, but after finishing, I thought perhaps it would be better to call and speak to him directly over the phone. Perhaps if he heard my voice and how unintimidating I really am, he might change his mind. But when I phoned, the warden refused to take my call. I spoke with his assistant, explaining my intentions—my heart—and asked if she might be able to convince the warden to at least hear me out. She agreed and took down my number.

A week later, the warden's assistant returned my call, telling me she had spoken to the warden about our conversation. She said there would be no need to discuss the matter further. The warden stood by his decision. Apparently there was some policy against victim-offender visitation. She told me something had happened in the past—someone had "ruined it for me."

I contacted just about everyone I could after that, trying to get the warden's decision overturned. Strategically working up the ranks, I called the warden's superior and then that superior's superior, and so on until I took it as far as I could. Some expressed appreciation for what I was trying to do, but ultimately I received the same response. The decision would remain.

With all options exhausted, it seemed this door would remain shut.

"We've hit a pretty significant roadblock," I wrote to Anthony. After explaining the situation, I said, "At this point, I think we just need to wait to see where this goes. I personally think that it'll take much prayer to come to where God wants this to go. I don't know what His plan is in all of this, but I do think He's up to something."

Anthony's response said he was saddened to hear that I had been turned down. He said, "I too believe God is working in our lives and in our situation. I believe if this is meant to happen, no person can stop it."

In my journal, I wrote:

Lord, I know You have Your timing. I know Your way is the best way. I just pray You open doors for me to see Anthony when it's the right time. Help me to be patient. Give me Your wisdom concerning this matter, and please put my heart at peace with the current circumstances. Please make Your way clear, and I will follow. I know it's presumptuous to ask, but please let me know if I will be able to go there at some point. I'm okay waiting, but I'd like to know whether or not I'm going to see him. I guess I just need to trust You—Your way, Your timing is perfect. Help me feel peace about it, my Lord!

The Bible tells us that God makes a way where there is no way.
I knew this was not over.

Chapter 8

THE PIECES

Anthony began to talk. Figuratively, I mean, through his letters. I thought maybe my denial had something to do with it, but I wasn't sure. He didn't answer any of the difficult questions I had asked about the day of the murder, but he did begin to share some of his story, and for that, I was thankful.

One thing that had always bothered me was Anthony's claim to faith. I couldn't seem to reconcile his claim with his actions. I didn't understand how he could claim to be a Christian at the time of the murder. I didn't see how a man could stand before his church, lead worship to a God he claimed to know and love—a God who is good and just—and less than a week later, intentionally drive to another man's house with a gun and kill him.

The dichotomy in Anthony's life screamed of hypocrisy.

I remember scoffing when I was told that Anthony had turned himself in to his pastor after the murder. His pastor was a guy named Ben. I didn't know Pastor Ben back then and had no real interaction with him until a few years ago, but I have since come to know Pastor Ben to be a godly man and a good pastor. Within a month of the murder, Ben had sent a letter to my family and me, expressing his condolences. He expressly stated that he and his church would not be assisting Anthony in any way and would do whatever necessary to ensure justice would be done. I appreciated the letter. But it left me confused.

A Christian murderer just didn't add up in my mind. It didn't add up then and, close to a decade later, it still didn't add up.

As a follower of Jesus, I understood that someone could come to Christ *after* committing murder—like Paul before his conversion on the road to Damascus or Moses before the burning bush. But how could someone, already claiming to know God, commit murder?

I talked to Pastor Bobby. I asked if it were possible for a Christian to commit murder. He told me it was and pointed me to David. After discussing the biblical story of David for some time, Bobby explained that, when someone gives their life to Christ, it does not mean they're immune to sin. He said that even though Jesus has given Christians victory over sin, sin is still a struggle, even for a true Christ follower. It didn't take much to see my own struggle with sin, and so I knew Bobby was right.

As Christians, we have been given the power of the Holy Spirit to attain sustainable victory over sin, but Christians are far from perfect. We are still prone to sin and desperately need God's grace to keep our hearts pure. Temptations still come, and if Christians don't continually guard and check their hearts they can fall to them. Becoming a Christian doesn't mean you have somehow "arrived" and will no longer do bad things. It simply means you have given your life to Jesus—that you have received God's forgiveness—and have allowed God access to your heart so that He can refine you into the image of His Son. And it's a process—one that takes a lifetime.

After considering all these things, I finally understood how it could be possible for someone to know God and commit such a terrible offense as murder. But here's the thing: not all people who claim to be Christians are. Some people call themselves Christians simply because their family took them to church as a child. Others go to church on their own but have never really given themselves to God.

To be a true Christian is to be a committed follower of Jesus. True Christians give their lives and everything they have and experience to God. True Christians believe with heart, mind, and soul that Jesus came, lived, died, and rose again on their behalf. This belief is so strong that it impacts their lives, causing them to think and act differently. It changes their whole existence, their whole being. This is what it means to be a true follower of Christ. It's not about whether you check the "Christian" box on a survey, but whether your belief is backed by the power of the living God.

This was my question. Was Anthony a true Christian or someone who simply checked the box? In his next letter, Anthony began to give insight. He wrote: "I'd like to say I was a Christian out there, I was not going through the motions. But I was under a lot of stress and pressure. . . . I was running on empty back then, and when I look back, I don't even know that person. It wasn't who I normally am. But I did what I did and must pay for that."

Anthony seemed to be transparent and honest, and I appreciated that. Considering his response, I wondered whether Anthony questioned the authenticity of his faith back then as well. It was hard to tell.

Anthony continued, writing about the relationship between his wife and my dad:

When I found out what was going on, I couldn't believe it. First I fell apart. . . . I blamed your dad . . . but I now know that sin causes us to do mean, even evil things. . . . I am so sorry that can't change what happened and it makes me feel even worse for what I did to Rick and your family.

Still, don't get angry, but your dad was doing wrong too. . . . The Bible warns us about adultery and how dangerous it is. I know why now. It's no excuse, I reacted wrongly. Had he and I loved our wives as Christ wants us to, this wouldn't have happened. I am so sorry.

I wasn't angry. I didn't like hearing about Dad's sins from Anthony, of all people, but he was right. I couldn't argue Anthony's point. Dad was wrong to begin a relationship with a woman who was still married.

When defining adultery* it seems people often rely on technicalities rather than absolute truths. Adultery is a sin that our society likes to define loosely. It seems each individual wants to subjectively define it to suit a personal agenda.

And I did it, too. I blurred the lines of adultery. I wanted to define it in a way that would paint my dad in the best light possible. I refused to admit that Dad was in any way at fault over the circumstances behind his murder because ultimately I felt that by admitting his fault, I would essentially be saying that what Anthony did was in some way justified. But it was not okay. It would never be okay. Murder can never be justified, regardless of the circumstances behind it.

Another person's sin is never justification for us to sin.

Additionally, I didn't want to admit Dad's fault because no one really knew the particulars about Dad and Diane's relationship. No one knew when their relationship began, and no one really knew whether they were intimately involved. When Dad told me about Diane, he told me that—even though they really liked one another—they had decided to wait until after Diane's divorce was finalized to pursue a relationship. I think he was trying to tell me that they weren't intimately involved. They still spoke on the phone to one another and saw one another on occasion, so there was definitely an inappropriate relationship going on, but Dad told me they were "playing it safe."

Yet the fact remains that when Dad began to build a new home for Anthony and Diane, both Dad and Diane were married to other spouses. Dad's divorce from the woman he married after Mom was

---

*As used herein, adultery has the meaning set forth in the Gospels by Jesus (see Matt. 5:27–30), which means lustful intent. References herein to "adultery" or "affair" do not imply any physical contact. Please see this book's postscript (p. 215).

finalized by the time he told me about Diane, but I don't know whether he began to see Diane before or after he filed for divorce.

Truly there are so many unknowns. Nobody really knows what happened. And it's beside the point, anyway.

Even before Anthony wrote this last letter, I knew I needed to stop rationalizing what had happened—or what may have happened. I needed to stop trying to paint a pretty picture in an attempt to gain approval for my dad from the world. And I needed to begin to see this situation as God saw it. Ultimately, it's not our definition of adultery that stands. God alone has the authority to define it, and Jesus said, "Everyone who looks at a woman with lustful intent has already committed adultery with her in his heart" (Matt. 5:28).

This was a hard pill to swallow.

I loved my dad. All I wanted to do was put on my rose-colored glasses and forget about the whole mess, but I couldn't. Dad's words—the ones he spoke to me shortly before his death—wouldn't let me. He had specifically told me not to idealize who he was after his death. Dad freely admitted that he had faults and asked me to do the same.

I struggled with this. I didn't want to remember his faults. I wanted to remember the good stuff. I wanted to remember how he'd wake us up at the crack of dawn to be the first on the lake to fish or in line at the ski lift. How he took me dove hunting when I was somewhere around ten years old with him and the guys. How he'd quickly shed his sweat-soaked shirt so that he could dive into just about every mountain lake we ever hiked to. Dad taught me to enjoy life. To work hard but to take time to play and have fun with family and friends. There really was so much good in my dad, but he was far from perfect.

Toward the end, Dad was in a bad spot. I thought it was strange that Anthony wrote, "When I look back, I don't even know that person. It wasn't who I normally am." I have said the same about my dad countless times. Perhaps they both found themselves to be punch drunk with stupidity and folly and sin at the same time, which ultimately created a perfect storm resulting in both death and destruction. I don't know.

What I do know is that the way Dad was at the end of his life was not who he normally was. I knew my dad to be an honest, kind, loving man. A man of integrity. But after Dad's father died, Dad turned inward and became extremely self-focused, seeking to do whatever he thought would make him happy. It seemed he was willing to seek happiness at all costs, even if his actions hurt others. But I don't think that was his intent. My dad was not mean spirited. He never intended to hurt others. He just did. It's like it was a by-product or consequence of securing his own happiness.

My dad was searching. He was looking to be filled. And just like so many other people, he believed the lie that wholeness can somehow come from things in this world—that relationships or money or stuff or status or food or achievements can somehow fill us. But they can't.

After twenty-two years of marriage to Mom, Dad left because he wasn't happy and spent the next five years searching for happiness through romantic relationships. When a particular relationship didn't bring him the happiness he thought it would—when it failed to fill him—he moved on, in the hope that the next one would be "it." But it never was because, you see, relationships were never intended to be our source of ultimate satisfaction. Relationships are a gift and a blessing from God, but ultimately, only God can satisfy us in the way our heart desires. Only God can fill us. Toward the end, I think Dad was beginning to understand this. He was seeking and coming to know God in a real way. By that time, though, he had already made a mess of things. He was already knee-deep in the muck and mire of sin.

For quite some time, I buried the reality of Dad's sins. I didn't want to see it, but as I wrestled through the reality of who my dad was—as I started to reconcile the good with the bad—I realized that I was no different. I remember praying for God to show me my sin for the first time the year before. The Bible says we all sin, so I figured I had to have sin in my life, but I didn't see my sin. So I prayed, and God answered. I think I spent the better part of three months in disgust of myself after that, crying out to God to change me, as the depths of my own depravity were revealed. I didn't like myself very much, but I knew I was forgiven. I knew God had chosen to love me and give me grace despite the sinful condition of my heart. God didn't abandon me because of my sin. He didn't look upon me with disgust, but with love. He gives grace and mercy, and we are to do the same.

One night as I was praying, it occurred to me that Anthony might not be the only one I needed to forgive. It seemed that I needed to forgive Dad as well, and I thought there might be others. I had never asked God to reveal any unforgiveness in my heart before, so I figured I ought to. In my journal, I wrote, "I know I have been forgiven much, so I am to forgive much. What am I holding on to?" I prayed, asking God to show me who I needed to forgive, and as I sat in bed with my journal upon my lap, God brought many people to my mind. I journaled about them all. Name after name was written down followed by the offense I had yet to forgive. I'd never thought I was the type of person to hold a grudge. Apparently I was.

As I finished writing my record of wrongs, I thought about just how ridiculous it was that I had held on to all of this for so many years. In my journal, I wrote:

Who am I to be holding on to all of this? I make mistakes. I'm sure many people could sit down and write a list of grievances they have with me from my past. I am not perfect, and neither are any of these people. . . .

It's our nature as fallen humans to have all these flaws, but my sins are horrendous! But the Lord Jesus said as He died on the cross, "It is finished." He has accomplished our salvation. He bore our sins—all of them. All of mine, all of those of these people. We are all forgiven; so too shall I forgive.

I proceeded to write, "Lord, I choose to forgive—" followed by every name and every offense I held on to. One by one, I brought each offense before God, asking for His strength to forgive, and I felt God release the resentment I had held for so long. Most of the issues I had were resolved rather easily—it didn't take much to see my folly in holding on to some of these relatively trivial offenses—but when I got to Dad, it was a different story. I held much more pain from my relationship with him than I had ever realized.

I poured my heart out to God. I knew I needed His strength not only to forgive, but also to heal from the wounds Dad had inflicted. I wrote:

Lord, I choose to forgive my dad! It was very hard when he left. It crushed my heart to have my daddy leave me and my family. Help me to forgive that he essentially became father only in name at that point in my life.

I know he was going through a lot emotionally, but what he did was not okay! Then to spend the next five years in sin, which led to his ultimate death. Dad had a hand in his own death. . . . Did he deserve to die? No, but he had a hand in it. Why would he be so stupid?

Lord God, please help me to forgive, truly forgive. I can only forgive within Your strength, Lord, so I ask for Your grace to allow me to forgive. Help my emotions, mind, and soul heal and come into line with my forgiveness.

I'd like to say that I forgave Dad and was healed instantly. I'd like to wrap this part of my journey up in a neat package tied up with a pretty little bow, but I can't. It wasn't easy like that. Healing took time, but ultimately it did come. It came over time as my eyes were opened to see my dad the way I now see all people, including myself—as a person desperately in need of God's grace. A man imperfect, yet loved by both God and me. I love my dad, and I know he loved me. And it turns out that's enough. Love is intended to be unconditional. That's not to say that we are to turn a blind eye to the sins of others, but we are to love as God loves, with a love that relentlessly pursues others despite their imperfections.

I guess what I'm trying to say is that I was able to forgive Dad and all those other people because I finally got to the point where I understood that we all stand in need of a Savior. I finally realized that I am no better than anyone else and that just because my sin may look different from the sins of others doesn't make my sin any better.

Sin is sin.

As I thought long and hard about that, it got me thinking about the sins I've committed against other people at one point or another. Up to this point, my focus had been on what others had done to me—how I've been wronged, how I've been the victim in some way or another—but I knew I had wronged my fair share of people as well.

God tells us to live peaceably with all—to forgive and to seek forgiveness. Those who follow Jesus have been given a message of reconciliation to share with this world, and how better to do that than by righting our wrongs?

Throughout the following weeks, I decided to contact each person I had wronged. Some were still in my life and were easy to contact. Others were more difficult and took some digging, but I found them all. One by one, I called or e-mailed or wrote or met for coffee to ask them for their forgiveness. It was a bit embarrassing and awkward to be contacting these people. Some of these issues stemmed from my high school days or before, and I didn't know if these people would even remember my wrongdoing. But I knew this is what God was calling me to. In the end, every person except one was receptive to my apology, and it seemed with each encounter that both of us left feeling a bit lighter. It's an amazing feeling to be at peace with people.

It had been a while since I received Anthony's last letter, but before I had a chance to write back, Anthony wrote again. He said, "I hope my last letter didn't offend or anger you. I'm real hesitant about opening up in a letter. So much can be lost or misread in translation. I was being honest with you about my frame of mind back then, but it's so hard to relate it to you cuz I hardly remember some of it. . . . I do hope I can one day sit down and really explain it all to you and apologize. Take care."

I figured I should write back. I didn't want my lack of response to be misread. I wasn't angry with him or anything. I was just a bit preoccupied with some of that other stuff.

It happened to be August 5, 2010. Ten years to the day since Anthony had taken my dad's life. I found it interesting that God had me write on that day of all days.

Ten years had passed. Ten years without my dad. Ten years since I had last heard his laugh or received one of his crazy hugs or seen the smile lines and the weblike wrinkles around his eyes deepen when he offered his joyful smile. I missed him terribly. On this day of all days, I missed him.

But for whatever reason, God had me writing. God had me living out His command to love Dad's murderer. And so I would choose not to wallow in all the pain this day brought to mind, and instead I would choose to love and move toward healing through forgiveness.

Once again, I sat at my computer—praying for God's words to flow through me—and wrote:

Dear Anthony,

. . . Your last letter didn't offend or anger me. On the contrary, I appreciate your honesty. I do know there are several versions to this story, and that's why I've asked for yours. I understand your apprehension to convey your story through a letter, but at this point, I think it's all we have. So, here's a little bit about where I'm at.

Though I've never been divorced, I somewhat understand the highly emotional state one can be in during a divorce because I closely witnessed those of some family members. It's hard. I get that. Additionally, I understand what it's like to be at rock bottom emotionally because I reached that point two years ago. It's essentially what God used to bring me to faith. That being said, by asking for your story, I'm truly just asking for better understanding. I believe God has made me go through certain things in my life since my dad's death in order to bring me to a place of greater understanding.

That's not to say that I will ever agree with what you did, nor will I ever say, think, or feel as though in any way it was okay or justifiable, for what was done was beyond words. It was tragic, it was horrific, it was an abomination in the sight of God, it was a sin, and for me it was devastating. Yet there still can be understanding.

Please don't read this letter as being hostile because I do not feel hostile when writing this. . . . I do recognize that my dad was committing adultery. He was not a perfect man. He made mistakes and he sinned, as we all do. . . .

. . . but I still don't believe my dad deserved to die the way he did. Though he was behaving wrongly, he was a kind, loving man who loved people. There is no justification for my dad's part in this, but he, too, was lost in a way. . . . He went down the wrong road, made bad decisions, and hurt people along the way. A while ago I was listening to a sermon that stated, "Hurting people hurt people," and I believe that to be true. Nonetheless, he was a great man with a great heart. He was a loving dad, and I miss him more than I can say. As I said before, though, my dad was wrong, and there is no justification for that either, just as there is no justification for your actions.

Ironically, I'm writing you on the tenth anniversary of my dad's death. While, in a way, it does get easier over time, there are wounds that run deep and have affected my entire being. I think God has me on this path in order to heal those wounds. I'm coming to a place of peace and forgiveness that can only be done through our Lord Jesus Christ. Though I'm not quite there yet, I believe God will bring me to that point someday.

On a side note, I was told that you may be opening another appeal. Is that true? Would you mind telling me about the appeal?

I hope this finds you well, and I'll let you know if I have any news on the possible visitation.

Sincerely,

Laurie

I was wrestling. There wasn't a moment of the day that I wasn't wrestling with one issue or another. If it wasn't with Dad's part in all this mess, it was with Anthony's. If it wasn't forgiving others, it was seeking forgiveness from others. It was a tumultuous time, but God was healing me. I could feel it. The change was subtle, but it was there. My perspective on just about everything was beginning to change, and my emotional response to Anthony seemed to be settling down. I began to see him in a different light and, though I was anything but sympathetic toward him, I thought for the first time that perhaps he had been just a regular guy who made a terrible, terrible decision. A man who, just like my dad and everyone else, was in desperate need of Jesus.

Chapter 9

CALM

I felt like Anthony and I were finally starting to get somewhere. It seemed both of us were committed to seeing where God would take this and were willing to do the work to get there. I saw this as evidence of God's grace because, after all, it isn't very often that you find two regular people who are willing to allow God to help them work through their differences, let alone two enemies.

After a few weeks had passed, I received Anthony's response to my letter:

Dear Laurie,

Hello. I pray you are well. I'm sorry I didn't write you right away, but I had to paint most of last week (my cell). Also my ninety year old grandmother came to visit. She's like four foot tall but still gets around.

I'd like to comment on your letter, to say it was inspiring is just not enough. Your compassion, grace, and mercy in this situation is truly inspiring and more than I deserve. Also, your grasp of Christ, His mission, His word, and His desire for our lives is more than people I know who've gone to church for years. To have come to your faith [less than] two years ago and be where you are now means two things, you read your Bible faithfully and you are going to a good church with a good pastor.

I too believe God will bring us face to face because what God wills man cannot stop. I think He may be working in your life to lead you into a ministry of helping others who have faced what you have. That brings me to saying that maybe one day when this warden leaves here you can reapply for visiting. I don't know what the questionnaire asks that they send you, and I don't want you to lie. But if they ask our relationship, maybe friend would be better. I leave that up to you.

You are totally right, your dad didn't deserve to die for having an affair,* and I'm truly sorry for what happened. The Bible is very clear about the risks of cheating with another man's wife, [P]roverbs is especially vocal about it. But I believe that is why it is so vocal, the emotions, pain, hurt, betrayal, revenge, so much floods your senses you can't think straight. I pray you never go through something like that. And nothing helps, you feel so damn alone. And the worst thing is that you feel abandoned by God. And you wonder what you could have done so bad that you deserve that.

I guess that's what they mean by living in a fallen world. I guess we are all fallen and capable of things we'd like to think we'd never do. That person I was on that day was only me for thirty minutes of my life and look at the damage it caused for a lifetime. I don't think I can apologize enough.

As for my appeal, it isn't a new one. I'll explain how it works, cuz believe me, I never knew how complicated our legal system was. You have two appeals basically. The first is a direct appeal, it goes right off the transcripts of the trial and is concerned only about legal errors. It goes directly to the Nevada Supreme Court. After they turn it down, and they will, then comes a post-conviction appeal. It has to do with errors your attorney committed. That goes back to the trial judge then

---

*Although Anthony maintains there was an "affair," Diane testified at the trial that there was no physical relationship between her and my dad, just as my dad had hinted to me. Please see this book's postscript (p. 215).

that one goes to the Nevada Supreme Court. After they turn it down, both appeals are combined and the appeal moves to the federal courts. That's where I am now. If they feel something is wrong they will send it back to the state courts to fix it. It's all a crap shoot so I can't tell you what may happen. I don't even know your feelings about it. You will have plenty of time to think about it though cuz it takes years to get a decision.

Well I guess I've written enough for now. Let me know if there is something else I can tell you. God bless Laurie, keep reading your Bible and keep that humble heart.

Sincerely,

Anthony

I hate to admit this, but my heart swelled with pride as I read this letter. Ridiculously prideful thoughts crossed my mind as I read—thoughts I didn't normally have.

Thoughts like—*I* am *being extremely compassionate and gracious and merciful. I am so glad Anthony understands that he doesn't deserve it!*

And—*I* do *know a lot about the Bible, more than a lot of other Christians I know.*

And the kicker—*I* am *humble.*

Now I was the hypocrite!

Anthony closed his letter by saying, "Keep that humble heart," but any humility I might have had prior to reading the letter had vanished completely. Why is it that humility is often negated by pride the moment it's praised? It's crazy how quickly we can fall to pride, or any other temptation for that matter. I suppose it's just part of our nature, something that proves our great need for a great God. A God who takes our ugly and makes it beautiful.

In the letter, Anthony addressed the possibility of reapplying for a visit in the future. He said, "If they ask our relationship, maybe friend would be better." Anthony had hit a nerve without knowing it.

First of all, I hated the word *relationship* being applied to Anthony and me. Every time I met with Pastor Bobby, I recoiled at the very thought of interacting with the man who had murdered my dad. I didn't want a relationship with this man. The way I saw it was that I was simply doing what God was calling me to do, and I hoped that didn't involve anything that could possibly be considered a relationship.

Second, though I know Anthony said he didn't want me to lie, he was suggesting I lie and call him a *friend*, of all things. *Friend!* Obviously, if the word *relationship* was so repulsive to me, the word *friend* would be even more revolting. Anthony was not my friend, and in my mind, he never would be. Additionally, those closest to me know that I quite literally cannot tell a lie. I can't even stretch the truth. More often than not, I end up sharing way too much information with people because I feel that if I don't tell a story in its entirety, I am in some way being deceptive. So obviously Anthony's suggestion was out of the question.

That being said, I didn't want to come across to Anthony as being hostile, and because of that I didn't think it would be a good idea to address my issues with him in my response. I figured they were relatively trivial issues. I didn't think Anthony meant any harm by what he was suggesting, anyway, so I figured it really didn't matter that much.

After a few weeks, I finally sat down and wrote:

Dear Anthony,

Thank you for your letter. I received it quite a while ago but haven't had a chance to respond until now. Unfortunately, nothing has changed on the visitation front (not that I anticipated it would), so there's nothing to report there. As far as reapplying once the current warden leaves, I guess we'll have to cross that bridge if or when it comes.

I do appreciate your honesty throughout your last letter. Thank you for explaining the appeal process to me. Though I did understand that most, if not all, convicts engage in an appeals process, I didn't know the intricacies of that process, so thank you. As far as my feelings about it,

I'm not angry that you're trying to appeal, but at the same time, to be perfectly honest, I would hope the courts would uphold your sentence given that I believe we all must face the consequences of our actions.

While I do recognize that you were in a difficult situation at the time, and you were out of sorts, you still did what you did and must pay the cost. Yet looking at the whole picture, including your side of the story, can provide understanding. As I may have written before, there is no justification for what you did, but there can be understanding.

Even though I believe you need to face your consequences, I do believe there can be forgiveness in situations like this. By that, I mean I believe there can be forgiveness from God if a person is truly repentant and has a complete change of heart, which only God can provide through His grace. I believe that person would have to be "washed," so to speak, and given both a clean heart and a right spirit by and through God's grace.

But in addition to the forgiveness of God, I believe there can be forgiveness from those affected by such tragedy (family members as well as other close individuals). Though forgiveness in a case such as this is difficult, and oftentimes, impossible, I do believe that it can be attained through God, and this is where I'm at. God has put me on this path toward forgiveness, and He's slowly healing me from this tragedy. Forgiveness, however, in no way is an act of condoning sins, for sin is never okay or justifiable, but instead it's an act of allowing oneself to heal. And true healing can only be given by God.

I do thank you for the insight you've provided thus far as far as what you were thinking at the time and where you were at. Any and all information helps to put the whole puzzle together, which leads to better understanding.

On a different note, it's interesting that you mentioned the ministry thing. Ever since I came to faith, I've had the same thought. I recently began a blog where I write posts pertaining to faith, God, and Jesus. . . . I don't know if it'll be helpful to others, but it's my hope that those who read it will be blessed by my experiences and thoughts. I truly believe that we're not called to believe for the sake of believing, or blessed for the sake of being blessed, but we are blessed so we can, in turn, be a blessing to others.

Anyway, I hope this finds you well, and I'll be praying that you continue to grow in your faith and can be a blessing within the prison.

Take care and God bless,

Laurie

I had written, "Forgiveness in a case such as this is difficult, and oftentimes, impossible," but this statement was only partially true. At the time, I mistakenly thought that forgiveness might not be possible in certain situations. But forgiveness is *always* possible; I just hadn't experienced it yet, and so it seemed like it might never happen. Without a doubt, I knew God *could* work forgiveness in me—I knew He was able—but when I was completely honest with myself, I had to admit that a small part of me still wasn't quite sure if He *would*.

I think I doubted God's will because forgiveness can seem like such an insurmountable task. Taking hold of forgiveness can seem like trying to contain water in your hands—it's difficult to grasp. But at the root of my doubt was fear. Deep down, I think I questioned, *What if God doesn't come through? What if I get to the end of all this, and I have nothing to show for it—I am none the wiser and still as messed up as ever? What if . . . ?*

Fear remained just below the surface, but I was determined not to allow fear or doubt to have any impact on the direction I was headed. If I was to err, I wanted to err on the side of faith rather than allow doubt to keep me from all that God has for me.

But still, the whole thing was just so strange. It was so weird to me that I was communicating with a man in prison who was painting his cell and having his four-foot-tall, ninety-year-old grandmother come visit. In the quiet moments of my days, I contemplated the path God set before me and thought, *My life is a bit odd*, as I smiled in anticipation of what I mostly knew God *would* do.

Chapter 10

FEAR

It was October. Five months has passed since I first began corresponding with Anthony, and for the first time I thought I might forgive him. I kept this to myself, though. I wasn't quite sure if my forgiveness was real, or if I only thought I forgave him. But I was changing. I didn't dislike Anthony as much as I had when we first began corresponding. He seemed sorry for what he had done, and for the first time, I thought maybe God had changed Anthony during the years he had spent in prison. Things seemed to be going well.

I was in a good place, and it seemed Anthony was, too.

I scheduled my nose surgery during the first week in October. I've always had trouble breathing through my nose, and even though it didn't seem to bother me much growing up, I figured it was time to fix it. But I dreaded the surgery. Those who had experienced similar surgeries told me the recovery would be awful, and, of course, that bit of information was anything but reassuring.

I drove to the surgery center in early morning darkness. I was feeling pretty nervous and began to pray earnestly for God to give me peace. Throughout my drive, I prayed for God to allow me to feel His presence—to know that I was being held in His mighty hand and that I was doing the right thing. I prayed that I would be okay. I knew without a doubt that God heard my prayers, and as I beseeched my God for a word, to my anxious heart He gently whispered, *Isaiah 43.*

I didn't know what Isaiah 43 said. I pulled out my iPhone, went to my Bible app, looked up Isaiah 43, and read the words God intended to encourage me with that morning. I read things like:

"Fear not."

"You are mine."

"I will be with you."

"The flame shall not consume you."

"I am the LORD your God, the Holy One of Israel, your Savior."

"You are precious in my eyes, and honored, and I love you."

Wow, I thought, somewhat in disbelief. *Really, God? Me?* In that moment, I experienced what the Bible describes as the peace that surpasses all understanding—*God's* peace. I got to the center and walked in for my surgery with not even an ounce of fear, not a hint of heaviness to my soul. I had no doubts about what I was doing. God had given me a message. I knew my standing before Him. I knew I was His, and I believed without a doubt that He would take care of me.

When other people told me the recovery would be terrible, I believed them, but I had no idea just how terrible it would be. The nose and sinus regions are apparently extremely sensitive, and when this area is in a lot of pain, it's kind of hard to think straight. So after the surgery, I was in bad shape—both physically and emotionally. The surgery rendered me weak, and it turned out to be the perfect time for Satan to mount an attack.

As I lay in bed the week after surgery, trying desperately to allow my body to heal, doubts began to flood my mind. I felt terrible, beyond anything I can even begin to describe, and to make matters worse, my anxiety had returned with a vengeance. It seemed fear had taken hold of me by the throat, once again, and I feared—with a fear better characterized by the word *terror*—that I'd end up right back where God had found me little more than a year and a half before.

Now, I'd like to tell you that I was an amazing woman of faith in this moment, but I wasn't. My trust in God began to wane as I wondered why He was allowing me to be in this terrible place. When God spoke Isaiah 43 over me, I thought He was telling me everything was going to be okay. I thought He would spare me from the fire, but apparently I misunderstood what God was trying to tell me. Isaiah 43:2 reads, "When you walk through fire you shall not be burned, and the flame shall not consume you." *When I walk through fire.* God knew what I was about to go through. He had prepared me for the fire, giving me a word before I even needed it to strengthen me in my moments of doubt.

Isaiah 43 became my lifeline over the next month as both my faith and my resolve to press on toward forgiveness were challenged. Like Jacob in the Bible, I found myself wrestling with God, and, as Jacob did, I refused to let go until God blessed me once again. I cried out to God, much like David did time and again throughout the Psalms, in the hope that He would pull me out of the mire once again. I wrote:

My Lord, my God—help! I'm overwhelmed by so much. . . . I'm a mess! Help me to trust You and believe Your Word—give me grace! I need You now. I am so very fearful! My anxiety is raging. . . . Calm my heart, calm my mind—save me once again from myself. . . .

I humbly admit that I need You—save me, my Lord. Save me. I am in desperate need of a Savior! Help me to learn to trust You in and through all things! Do not let me return to my Egypt—to that deep dark place You once found me! Bring Your light and shine it in the darkest places within. Heal me—bind my wounds and bring me to wholeness!

I love You and I need You and I choose to trust You! I choose to trust You.

Trusting God in this moment was a choice. I didn't feel trust, but I *chose* trust.

Anthony wrote that week. It was terrible timing. At least that's how I saw it back then. The last thing I wanted to deal with was Anthony.

Travis brought me the letter; when he did, I was sitting in my bed, propped by pillows, with a ridiculous contraption designed to catch blood and whatever else dripped from the thing on my face that only remotely resembled a nose. I was in a lot of pain. I was grumpy. My faith was being challenged. And I was extremely nervous and fearful— not the ideal time to read a letter from the man who murdered my dad. And I knew it. As soon as the letter was given to me, I set it aside and tried to ignore it, but it's kind of hard not to read a letter like this. So I ended up giving in after only a few minutes.

The letter read:

Dear Laurie,

Hello. How are you? I got your letter. Sorry it's taken a while to respond. Because of state furloughs we have been locked down a lot. That stopped three weeks ago so I've been busier. I've been able to go to church again, work out and just go outside.

I'm glad you have been led by God to this ministry. . . . I believe God has led me to a music ministry. I play on our church choir and write songs, several songs. I'm enclosing one for you.

I understand your feelings on my sentence. I, of course, don't share them. I'm hesitant to go here but we have been honest with each other to this point so I'm not changing that. I was offered second degree by the D.A. before the trial. That would have made me eligible for parole in ten years. I felt it was manslaughter, due to the circumstances, that would have made me eligible in maybe two more. Also at my last hearing the trial judge told me and the court he didn't think it was a first degree case.

I am in here with people who killed someone for no reason, or drugs or killed two people and have less time than me. I don't think that's justice. I am sorry. I respect your feelings and don't blame you for having them.

I, like you, believe God can and will work a miracle in our situation. Forgiveness will free us both to be better people and fulfill God's will for our lives. But I won't lie, I hope one day to go home and record the music God has put in my heart. I believe he has gifted me in this area to share with others, even if it's only a few. I hope this doesn't upset you, I'm not trying to. I just want to share what I believe God wants me to.

Thank you, take care.

God bless,

Anthony

I was feeling a bit sassy. Anthony said he wanted to share what he believed God wanted him to, and I was pretty sure I knew why—so I could set him straight! One thing was clear—things were about to get heated.

Anthony's logic was just so twisted. I could not believe he was trying to justify his actions by saying: "I am in here with people who killed someone for no reason, or drugs or killed two people and have less time than me. I don't think that's justice." *Really?* I thought. *Because the last time I checked, God's justice for murder is death—not twenty years in prison, not even life without parole, but death.* Anthony suggested that having a *reason* for murdering someone is better than not having a reason at all— as if having a reason for intentionally taking a life deserves a lesser sentence. Murder is murder. No one murder is better than any other.

Even if we were grading murder on a scale here—which we're not— it's not as if Anthony walked in on Dad and Diane in one another's arms and killed Dad in the heat of passion. No. Anthony's actions seemed to be planned. He had been seen outside Dad's house numerous times in violation of a restraining order prior to the murder and had deliberately driven to Dad's house with a gun the day of the murder—after having bailed himself out of jail for violating the order once again—and my dad ended up dead. Anthony claimed he only wanted to "talk" to Dad, but obviously that didn't happen.

This letter clearly indicated to me that Anthony was not repentant. He seemed to be remorseful—he seemed to regret what he had done, but I did not think he was repentant. Repentance requires us to take complete ownership of our sins. We don't get to justify our behavior or shift blame or squirm our way out of consequences. We may have reasons behind our actions, but no reason can be used as justification for our sins.

I was angry. Evidently, the forgiveness I thought I had come to was only a mirage.

A few days later, I received another letter from Anthony. He said:

Dear Laurie,

How are you? You're probably surprised to hear from me. I wanted to clarify something from my last letter. I may not feel it is just, compared to others here, but I am willing to spend the rest of my life in prison if it's God's will for me to do so.

Here's the thing, when I was out there I thought our justice system worked so well. I even voted for the life without law I'm sentenced under. But now that I'm in here, I feel our justice system is broken. I have been and am locked up with men, as I said, who have done terrible things and have less time. I'm locked up with men who I believe are innocent, one, a friend, was just let out after nine years, wrongly accused. And no one cares, not lawyers, judges or society. Lock us all up and forget them. It's an attitude that so many have.

Now don't get me wrong a lot deserve to be here. But some committed their crimes when they were so young and are completely different people. Yet a dysfunctional parole board will not give them a chance or they get a chance and the system never taught them a skill so that they could work and feed themselves. Prison doesn't teach them any job skills and now with budget shortages they are even cutting their classes. The sad thing was they never offered all the classes for a degree. Maybe if you were here for ten years! I'm sorry I'm ranting, this place makes me angry or I should say the injustice makes me angry.

God gives us all ministries. I've often thought if I was ever released I would work with released inmates. I offered to teach a plumbing course that would give an inmate a year's apprentice experience but was shot down. As I said I also want to record my songs. Those are hopes and prayers, maybe not reality. I know you'd probably rather see me stay here. I can understand that. But maybe on this path of forgiveness one day you won't feel as strongly about it. I know it may never go away, I don't expect it too, I just hope, well, I don't know what I hope. I guess I hope for peace for both of us and for God's will in our lives to be fulfilled. I do pray the best for you Laurie, I truly do and will forever be sorry for what I did and how I hurt your family.

Sincerely,

Anthony

P.S. Thanks for listening, sorry to have bothered you so soon.

After five months of correspondence, I thought I was beginning to know Anthony, but these letters revealed a whole new side that I had yet to see and, quite frankly, it scared me. I began to question whether Anthony and I were headed in the right direction. I felt like we were getting too chummy. *What was I doing writing all that stuff about ministry and serving God?* I thought. *That's the kind of stuff you talk about with those you're close to. This was Dad's murderer, for goodness' sake.*

So many stories tell about inmates conning people and, out of nowhere, I began to fear Anthony might be trying to deceive me. I didn't know this man. We had exchanged quite a few letters at this point, but I didn't know what he was capable of. Certainly, a man capable of murder is not to be trusted. Then one day, a thought struck me:

Crap! What if he tries to use what I've already written in his appeal? I certainly didn't want to be the one responsible for setting the man who murdered my dad free. I thought maybe I had been a fool.

I put Anthony's letters on my nightstand, a place out of the way but visible. I didn't know how to proceed. I knew if I were to go with my initial response, it would be more reactive than responsive, and that was not what I was called to. I decided to sit on these letters and wait for God to show me how to respond. Each time I passed the letters on my nightstand, they reminded me to pray—to seek God and His will. I prayed for wisdom, for guidance, for protection, and for the ability to discern whether or not Anthony was being straight.

I was struggling, but not just with Anthony. I was still wrestling through the storm that began the moment I woke from surgery. This season of my life was quite possibly the most difficult season I had experienced since giving my life to Jesus. The recovery from surgery was painfully difficult, but the physical pain had nothing on the emotional and spiritual storm that raged within my heart and mind.

I let over a month pass before responding to Anthony. By this time, the storm had lessened. It was still there but, as I had wrestled alongside God throughout that month, I had been given clarity on how to respond. I felt it was important to be gracious but completely honest. Anthony wouldn't like what I had to say, but I felt God was calling me to honesty anyway.

Sitting at my computer, I said one last prayer and wrote:

Dear Anthony,

  After receiving your last two letters, I've had to do a lot of thinking.

  While I'm not angry with you for what was said, I have a general feeling of discomfort and uneasiness about where this is going. It has never been my intention, nor is it now, to befriend you, yet I do believe God calls us all to be kind and loving to all, so that has been and continues to be a goal of mine in regard to our correspondence.

I began this journey because I felt God was leading me toward forgiveness, and I do believe God will help me to attain this regardless of what transpires. Yet, I now find myself in this situation where I am beginning to question your goals, motivations, and/or genuineness in our correspondence. Frankly, I am beginning to question whether or not you have ulterior motives for corresponding with me, which could have to do with your desire to attain your freedom. Basically, I wonder if there's a bit of manipulation going on here, and I question whether or not you'll use what I've said in my letters in your appeal.

The reasons behind these feelings have to do with several different aspects to our correspondence that I've been noticing. One is that I, long ago, asked you the questions that I have pertaining to your side of the story. I truly feel that answers to these questions could help me to see the big picture more clearly, yet you decided not to share, stating that we could discuss these if we were able to meet. After my application was denied, I once again alluded to the fact that more information would be helpful, but once again it wasn't addressed. While I understand reluctance due to not wanting information to be misconstrued, I wonder how much of your denial to answer these questions has to do with not wanting to put incriminating information down on paper. Essentially, this is one of my reasons for the lack of trust.

Additionally, while you have said that you will "forever be sorry for what [you] did and how [you] hurt [my] family," your last two letters seemed to indicate that you're justifying your actions by claiming you had a "reason" for killing my dad. While I will never dispute the fact that my dad made some mistakes, there is absolutely no justification for what you did, and the fact that you had a "reason" for committing murder doesn't make your actions any more or less of a crime. And having a "reason" doesn't make it any more okay than those who committed murder for no apparent reason.

As far as the injustice of the prison system goes, I don't doubt that it's an imperfect system, and I'm sure reforms are needed. I agree that prisoners should be taught a skill, so they can be productive members of our society upon release. I, too, agree that mistakes are made, and that prisoners can be wrongly accused and convicted. It is a shame! Our society should care more about the failures of the prison system. Yet, I personally don't believe any of that has to do with you and your sentence. You did commit premeditated murder.

Since becoming a Christian, I've looked a lot into what the Bible says about murder (as I'm sure you're familiar with yourself). Murder, under the old covenant, was punished by death unless it was an accident, which was not the case in your scenario. The new covenant says next to nothing about the sentencing of murder, yet I do recognize that Jesus came to save anyone willing to repent of their evil and commit their lives to Him. What's prominent, however, is that all those in earthly authority (kings, rulers, judges, etc.) are placed there under the authority of God. Consequently, we are to submit to their rulings and/or judgments. God is sovereign over all, and even if there are mistakes made by those in authority, God is sovereign, so no ruling can be made without His approval.

That being said, one more thought that I have has to do with comparing ourselves to others. I think this is dangerous, yet I believe we all do it to a certain extent. In [your] case, you seem to be comparing the sentence you received to others' sentences, and you find it unfair and unjust. One thing to consider is that we, as Christians, are not to judge ourselves based upon those around us. Many of us look around and consciously or unconsciously compare ourselves to others in the world. We look around and see that there are people out there who have done x or committed y, then we look to ourselves and say, "[W]ell, I haven't done that, so I'm a pretty good person." Yet, the Bible teaches us that none are good. That we have all turned away from God, and were, at one time, enemies of God—our creator. We are reminded to be in the world, but not of the world. That we are different, and that we not think more highly of ourselves or our actions than we ought. When comparing your sentence in relationship to your crime to that of those around you, what you're essentially saying is that God isn't in control of your situation; that He didn't oversee your sentence. That because you had a "reason" it's somehow better than not having a reason. That you deserve less time because my dad got you really mad?!? As if that's justification!

As mentioned, God is in control of all of this. If He wills you to be free, you will be set free. If you were supposed to take the plea bargain offered for second degree, you would have, but you didn't because it wasn't God's plan, just as your sentence was God's will.

So, my question for you is this . . . what are your motives? What do you want out of our correspondence? And I'd like to humbly challenge you to pray to see your situation through God's eyes. I've been praying for this on my end, and I truly believe He's been answering my prayers. I've been asking Him to allow me to view the entire situation through the lens of the gospel, not through the lens of the victim's daughter, which brings with it much biases and baggage, and boy, have my perceptions changed!

Additionally, I invite you once again to answer my difficult questions. I realize that they're difficult. I realize that things can be misconstrued through the written word, but I believe all that can be ironed out if we both rely on Christ through this. If you'd like a reminder of what questions I have, I've pasted my previously written questions below. It reads:

As you know, I attended your trial every day, so I know what was said there. What I would like to ask you, though, is for your story. Much light was shed on this topic during the trial, but I'd like to have your perspective. How did this happen? Why did this happen? What led you to this point? What really went on in my dad's house on August 5th? What was the tone of your conversation? What was said (on my dad's part as well as yours)? What set you off? Did my dad say something before you shot him? What were my dad's last words? I'm not asking for you to justify what you did because what you did can never be justified, and it will never be okay. But I do realize that you have insight into the situation that I have yet to hear. As much detail as you can provide would be much appreciated.

I know that I've been brutally honest throughout this letter, but I feel honesty is the best way to go. It is not my desire to anger you, nor am I consumed with any anger toward you. Additionally, my desire for you to spend the rest of your life in prison has nothing to do with any desire to see you suffer, I simply believe that you should face the consequences for your actions, just as we all must.

I hope this finds you well. I'll be praying for God's will in this, and for peace for both of us.

Take care,

Laurie

Anthony's response came within the week. As predicted, he didn't like what I had to say:

Dear Laurie

I just received your letter and many of my concerns about writing were confirmed. First, I can't imagine what I could have written that would have led you to believe I was manipulating you. And second, at no time did it enter my mind to use anything you have written me to my advantage, in my appeal, or in a courtroom. In fact I tore up your letters so there'd be no fear of them being used. And an appeal is a legal document concerning what happened at trial and what the attorneys may or may not have done.

You speak of trust, well trusting you is very hard for me. I trusted someone I thought was a strong Christian woman and look at what happened. I know you aren't Diane but I'd like to make an observation. Before I killed your dad, who were the victims? [Your dad's ex-wife] and me. We were the ones betrayed and lied to. I am not trying to justify what I did, but you bring up [Old Testament] law for murder, well what is the punishment for adultery? Death to both parties involved. No, I do not plan nor did I ever, of hurting Diane. And I did not plan your dad's death either. I have never said I had a "reason" for killing your dad but you wanted to know what led up to that day, what was my emotional state and such. I felt it was safe to give you an overview of the stuff leading up to it. This also seems to have been misconstrued as justification, not so.

You were right though in saying we Christians are held to a higher standard, and I am wrong to compare my sentence to others. But you also said it was God's will that I not accept the plea deal. We are not mindless creations that God uses in a cosmic chess game. We are his creations and we do things every day (all day) that are against His will. I can tell you this with certainty, it was not God's will that Rick and Diane were unfaithful to their spouses and it was not His will that I went over to your dad's house that day. It may not even be His will that I spend the rest of my life in prison, but that doesn't mean I won't.

Even as Christians we rebel against God, we grieve the Holy Spirit, we sin. In this life we will never be perfect, but in the one to come, you and I will be brother and sister, as much as you may hate that now.

You ask what are my motives, I don't have any, I didn't initiate our correspondence, but I think I want the same as you, understanding and forgiveness. You want answers to things I haven't thought about in years, and to tell the truth I don't want to. But Laurie in order to trust you I want to know some things. Do you want to know so that you can use it against me? Will it come up in court? Or is this something you believe will bring you peace, because I am skeptical that it will bring you that peace. But I will pray about this and I ask you to do the same. My grandmother is here till Thanksgiving so I hope to know by the time she leaves. Write me then, and know this if I do this it will be against the wishes of my attorney and my family, so please be trustworthy. I hope this letter hasn't sounded too harsh, I haven't meant it to be. In my heart

I truly want to answer all your questions, I do want forgiveness and for you to find peace.

Take care.

Sincerely,

Anthony

If Anthony wanted me to believe he didn't plan the murder, he was going to have to prove it to me. In my mind, the murder was obviously no accident. Who in his right mind would take a gun to a man's house just to point it at him after driving by the man's house over and over, as if stalking prey, days and weeks prior to the murder? I didn't believe for one moment that Anthony didn't intend to kill my dad.

Anthony had made some good points in this letter about some of the other stuff, though. I hated to admit it, but he was right about Old Testament law for adultery. He was right that we aren't God's pawns. And even though the very thought of it made me shudder, he was right that he and I would most likely stand together to worship Jesus for eternity.

Anthony and I were now knee-deep in the muck. Apparently all that nice, surface-level stuff was a thing of the past. I didn't like that it was getting heated—and frankly I wondered if it was wise to make a murderer mad—but it seemed to me that it's often necessary to wallow in the muck for a while to come out clean on the other side.

God had led me into this fire. I knew He was with me, and as promised in Isaiah 43, I would not be burned—these flames would not consume me. This would merely be a walk through the fire, and I'd most assuredly come out unscathed, and perhaps even better than I had entered it.

Chapter 11

TENSION

I was starting to feel like a normal person again. I still had some healing to do six weeks post surgery, but I was pretty sure I could conquer anything with my emotions and anxiety in check, and they were. God had pulled me through but, to be honest, I was a little shell-shocked—a little baffled. When I woke from surgery, I was not okay. I was fine one moment, and then completely not fine the next. But as I emerged out of that fire, one thing was perfectly clear—it was by God's grace alone that I was emotionally, physically, and spiritually stable.

It got me thinking about Anthony. Perhaps God had allowed me to fall so I could come to understand both the frailty of man and the power of God's saving grace. Perhaps I needed to understand just how quickly one can fall, or maybe even how Anthony could have fallen. I thought about all Anthony had shared about his frame of mind back then—I thought about all I had gone through over the years, all the pain and brokenness—and for the first time, I realized that perhaps the line between Anthony and me was thinner than I had ever imagined.

John Bradford, who was imprisoned and martyred for his Protestant faith in sixteenth-century England, reportedly said, "There, but for the grace of God, goes John Bradford," each time he watched his fellow inmates being led toward their execution. It seemed Bradford may have understood something I was only beginning to grasp—that apart from God's grace, we are all capable of doing the unthinkable.

Maybe that was the key. Perhaps humbly accepting our propensity to sin is the very thing that protects us from sin. Maybe recognizing our proclivity toward sin is what enables us to keep a humble heart. To judge ourselves with sober judgment. To not think more highly of ourselves than we ought. All of which should drive us to God. When we rightfully believe we're capable of doing things we never thought we could, we begin to understand our need for God's amazing grace. Paul wrote to the church in Corinth, "By the grace of God I am what I am" (1 Cor. 15:10), and he was right. It is by grace alone that we stand.

That I stand.

These thoughts swirled around my mind for days. It seemed I was getting it, but I still felt like something was missing. As it would turn out, that something would be a doozy.

I got distracted as I was reading my Bible one morning. I started to think about Anthony's last letter and how I might respond. Then God whispered, *You are no better than him.* The words hit me square in the face, and I'm pretty sure I literally flinched when I heard them. I wasn't quite sure what to do. I knew I was capable of the unthinkable—God had already established that—but I hadn't actually done the unthinkable. Shouldn't that count for something? Doesn't that make me better than someone who has actually done it?

We all seem to have our own opinion about sin. Setting God's Word aside, we seem to classify sin or put it into some subjectively based, self-construed hierarchy. We like to think that a lustful thought is better than adultery. That hatred for another is better than murder. Or that things like gossip, lying, anxiety, unthankfulness, pride, selfishness, impatience, and lack of self-control are somehow better than more grievous sins—and, in a sense, they are. Admittedly, some sins are less consequential than others, but as I looked at this issue—as I sought to understand what God was trying to show me—I suddenly understood that God doesn't see sin as we see sin.

Sin is no trivial matter to God. Every sin we commit is active rebellion against Him. It's an attempt to do things our way. To live apart from God. Autonomy is the aim behind every sin—whether we're conscious of that fact or not—and God cannot stand for that. He knows a life apart from Him leads to complete and total destruction. A life apart from God results in an eternity apart from God, which is something that breaks His heart.

God loves us entirely too much to allow us to live apart from Him, which is why He provided a way out of all this mess. The moment we come to Christ by faith, we are washed clean—freed from our bondage to sin. But as Paul pointed out, "There is no distinction: for all have sinned and fall short of the glory of God, and are justified by his grace as a gift, through the redemption that is in Christ Jesus" (Rom. 3:22–24).

There is no distinction.

It's not every day you're told you are no better than a murderer, but I knew God was right. I mean, of course He was right—He's God!

It appeared Anthony and I had both given ourselves to Jesus. We were both equally sinners in need of grace. We were both washed clean. Before our God, we stood on level ground, equally loved and forgiven. It was a difficult truth to swallow, but God's Word was clear. I am no better than Anthony.

With that in mind, I sat down to respond. We still had many issues to work through, but God had given me a perspective that I would need for what was to come. With Anthony's last letter sitting on my desk before me, I wrote:

Dear Anthony,

I don't know how to start this other than to just dive in.

For clarification's sake, it was "safe" to give me an overview of the events leading up to my dad's death. I didn't get the sense that you were justifying your actions until your last two letters when you were comparing your circumstances to those around you. Therefore, I did not take your overview of events prior to the murder as justification, so nothing was misconstrued as far as that was concerned.

As far as our trust issue goes, what you have to understand is that you are my dad's murderer. There's an element of distrust that goes along with the territory. Additionally, I don't know you. I don't know what you're capable of, yet I do know that you are, or were at one point, capable of murder. I would like to trust that you are a changed man. That you have been transformed by the gospel, as I have been, yet the nature of our relationship lends itself to my need to protect myself.

That being said, I think it's fair to answer my own questions I asked of you, as you deserve to protect yourself as well. My motivations behind our correspondence come from the desire to gain insight and understanding and ultimately peace with my past. My dad's murder has truly transformed my life in so many ways. The scars run deep, and I know that only God can heal me from my past. Essentially, I truly believe God set me on this path for this purpose: to forgive, to heal, and to bring peace perhaps to both of us. I have absolutely no desire to harm you in any way. That being said, I have absolutely no desire to use any of what you have said or will say against you in any way. Personally, I think that would be deceitful and dishonest, which God would not look kindly on.

As for my desire to know more, there's so much about my dad's last moments that I don't know. I know that receiving this information initially will not bring me peace, but not knowing has also left me without peace. I do believe that it'll be hard to hear what really went on, yet at the same time, I think that it'll allow me to heal more completely over time. Will it hurt me? Absolutely, but I know that God will bring good out of it, just as He does all things! Through pain are we molded. Through suffering we are more malleable in God's hands. That being said, if you choose to tell me more about what happened on August 5, 2000, I pray that you don't spare the details. In my mind, this event is [chock-full] of holes at this point, and I believe that's part of what's holding me back from reaching complete healing and peace about the situation.

In reference to Old Testament law regarding adultery, you are right. As we've written on before, sins were committed on both sides, but what I think we must all be careful of is justifying our sins. That is to say, I sinned as a response to your sin, so it's somehow justifiable. If we're sinned against, we're called to man up, be humble, and turn the other cheek.

You mentioned that you and [my dad's ex-wife] were victims prior to killing my dad. That is true, but I'm sure there are two sides to both of these stories. I'm sure that you weren't the sole victim nor was [my dad's ex-wife]. Through closely witnessing another family member's divorce, I can say that it takes both parties within a marriage to break it up even if one doesn't initiate the separation. Frankly, I believe you were all victimizing each other to various degrees. You and [my dad's ex-wife] were the victims, but within each of those marriages, much was going on that "victimized" all of those involved. None of you were innocent! You were all guilty of wrongdoing and sin throughout the entire ordeal. The saddest part of all, however, has nothing to do with any of you! The biggest victims of all are always the innocent children that are involved. They're the real victims!

Additionally, you mentioned that you didn't plan on killing my dad. I think that if you want me to believe you in this area, you're going to have to give me more information. The way I see it is that you may not have planned on going through with the murder months/weeks prior to the event, but you did plan on killing him at the very least on the day of the murder (which is still premeditated murder)! Additionally, even if you weren't going around planning the murder long before it occurred, you still cultivated the emotions, feelings, etc. that [led] you astray. You still allowed your soul to be poisoned with hatred, which ultimately led to your actions.

I agree with the fact that we're not pawns in God's hands. We do all have free will, and we do choose to rebel against God all the time, yet at the same time, the Bible clearly states the fact that God is sovereign over all, and that He can and does choose to stop us from sinning against Him. Consequently, He is all-powerful and in control of all things. Any sinning that we do, He allows for His purposes and His glory. I believe He uses sin/tragedy/disasters for His purposes and to display His might and glory. Though, I also recognize that He does not will us to sin. It does grieve Him! I do not believe any of what happened back in 2000 was His will, but He has used it for His purposes. The Bible says that God never tempts us to sin, so it is not His will, BUT He does allow it and He does use it for His purposes. Romans 8:28 says that He works all things for good for those who love Him (paraphrased), and He is doing that in our situation as well. Perhaps He allowed you to sin and wind up in prison in order for you to bring other inmates to Him and bring Him glory. In my case, I don't know that I would have turned to Christ without my dad being murdered, and I have come to a desire to impact the world for Christ. There are other dimensions I could develop in this area, but that would take way too long. I think you get my point. Essentially, nothing is surprising to God. Your actions didn't surprise Him, and in fact, while He didn't will you to sin, He did allow it.

All this being said, one thing that God's been working on me with lately is the fact that I am no better than you or any other sinner out there. As mentioned in my previous letter, I think we all want to compare ourselves to others to feel better about ourselves, to somehow believe that we're "good people," but as the Bible says, none is good, we have all turned away. Nonetheless, I maintain my position that we all must face the consequences of our actions.

Since I've asked for your story, I think it's fair to include mine. Perhaps if I share my blog post about my experience on August 5th, it'll help you in your quest for peace.

I'll be praying about all this, as I have for a long time now.
Take care and God bless,
Laurie

As I wrote this letter, I began to have a greater understanding of what I was asking of Anthony. I was asking a lot. I was asking him to go back to the worst day of his life, for me. To unearth things I knew he'd rather leave buried. To answer questions he did not want to answer. And it seemed to me that I ought to do the same. I had asked for Anthony's story, and it was only fair that I share mine as well.

I started to dabble in the blogging world right before I began to correspond with Anthony. I had written a blog post about the murder shortly thereafter and figured the easiest, most effective way to share my story with Anthony was to include that post with my letter.

I hoped this letter would ease the tension between Anthony and me. I hoped it would allow us to continue to move toward forgiveness and healing. I wanted so desperately to honor God with my words—to speak truth, to be merciful and gracious—and I honestly thought this letter would achieve those ends. I thought this letter would settle some of the issues Anthony and I had with one another. But after receiving Anthony's response, I realized I was wrong.

The response, which came three weeks later, was nothing like the response I had anticipated. He wrote:

Dear Laurie,

   Sorry it took so long to write back. I haven't slept much since your last letter, and I wasn't sure I would write back. First I'd like to address your letter then "your story." I understand your trust issues, you don't know me. And after reading "your story" I don't think you want to. You are also correct in stating both parties in our marriages hurt each other. But as far as I'm concerned adultery is never justified. It is the lowest form of betrayal. You are also correct in stating that I may have cultivated the emotions that led me to be poisoned. But not hate, anger yes but I didn't hate your dad. I did not go over to your dad's house to kill him, to threaten and scare, yes. But having that anger in my heart opened me up to the possibility of something bad and as we know bad happened.

Now as for "your story" or what started out as your story and then digressed into an indictment of me, well I was hurt and saddened. No where did I read your dad's name or Diane's only my full name three times. I don't even go by Anthony but Tony and to use my last name knowing I have family who are out there . . . who did nothing wrong and now to have this brought out to the internet, no less, and have to deal with it all over. . . .

And then to read all Diane's regurgitated lies about me and our marriage leads me to believe you don't want to know the truth. . . . I am not trying to diminish my responsibility in your dad's death, he died at my hands. But Diane's hands dug his grave. . . .

. . . Well I'd like to tell you, I haven't lied to you, I've got nothing to gain, [Diane] wants your acceptance, I don't. And what did all that garbage have to do with your story anyway. It lends nothing to your story. In fact, you said there are two sides, but you have chosen which one to believe. Therefore, you are also lying about me, and I don't believe we can go any further in our correspondence out of respect for my family. I'd like my last name removed, and out of respect for the truth, I'd like but you can choose to remove Diane's crap.

Before this letter, I prayed for forgiveness between Diane and I, and as for me, I felt it was happening. But reading all that just brought all the hurt back in full force. I guess I have to work on it. No where did you write about us building a bridge of trust and forgiveness. And now it is gone. Maybe we can start again someday, but not as long as that, as written stays posted. Sorry, I truly am.

Sincerely,

Anthony

Who the hell does he think he is? I thought. Anthony was shifting blame, pointing fingers like a child saying, "She did it first!" I couldn't believe what I read. Anthony had written only a few sentences addressing my letter—a letter that I thought was kind and gracious—but spent the next five pages ripping apart my story, telling me I was wrong.

I was willing to admit that my story was biased, but Anthony had a lot of nerve. He had every right to disagree with what I wrote—and even cordially correct my errors—but in my estimation, he had absolutely no right to get angry at my story, regardless of who or what may have influenced my thinking.

It probably should have scared me that I had made this man so mad, but it didn't. I wasn't scared; I was angry, and a bit disgusted as well. I had given this man grace time and time again since we began our correspondence months ago. He had said many things that made me angry, giving me every opportunity to treat him poorly, but I hadn't—I intentionally tried to give grace instead. But apparently, Anthony wasn't willing to do the same. It seemed Anthony had given me an ultimatum in lieu of grace—he seemed to be telling me, "Change your story or we're through"—and that did not sit well with me.

I called my girlfriend Sarah. This wasn't the first time she'd had to talk me down. Sarah had been walking with me through this journey since the beginning and had always been there to give me solid, biblical advice. She had read all the letters, both mine and Anthony's, and was well aware of what had been going on up to this point.

"I got another letter," I said when she picked up.

"What'd he say?"

"Listen to this," I said. I began to read. I read the letter with a bit of flair as Sarah listened intently on the other side, interjecting with *what?* and *really?* in all the right spots.

"I can't believe he said those things," Sarah said when I finished.

"I know!" I said with quite a bit of sass. "He's still doing it. He's still justifying. Still blame shifting. Why won't he simply say '*I* did it. It was *my* fault. Period.' He's still trying to justify his actions. He committed murder! He killed my dad! There's absolutely no justification for that!"

Sarah agreed.

I continued my rant. "Can you believe he said that Diane dug my dad's grave?"

"That's crazy."

"It is, isn't it?" I said. "He's not repentant. He can't be! Repentance requires one to actually take responsibility for their own actions, and Anthony's certainly not doing that!"

Sarah and I spoke a little while longer before I told her I had to go. I wanted to reread the blog post I had sent to Anthony to see what set him off. In hindsight, I should have read it before I sent it to him, but I hadn't read that post since it was written less than a year before. I thought maybe I had made a mistake.

But, then again, maybe I hadn't. As I read the post, I didn't see anything outlandish in my story. It was biased, for sure, but I thought biases would be a given in a situation like this. Truthfully, the only thing I probably shouldn't have written was Anthony's full name. There were some other things in the post I would change now, since God had allowed me to see things a bit differently, but the post was a complete reflection of how I saw the murder prior to corresponding with Anthony. As I looked at the post, I decided I ought to remove Anthony's name, though I kept the rest pretty much the same. I didn't want to edit it even if I did find an error in the post. I didn't want Anthony to think he could tell me what to do. It was childish, I knew, but I was feeling a bit spiteful. I was not about to take an ultimatum from the man who had murdered my dad.

After I looked at the post, I began to write my response to Anthony. He needed to be set straight—he needed a good old-fashioned rebuke, in my mind—and I was willing to give him one. This man claimed to be a Christian; I figured it was about time he acted like one.

I addressed each of the issues Anthony had set forth in my response.

I wanted to put this blame-shifting nonsense to bed. I wanted Anthony to know that he was solely responsible for Dad's death. That he, and he alone, murdered my dad. I thought I needed to make this perfectly clear, and so I addressed this issue in the letter by saying, "You, in fact, are the one who decided to bring the gun over there. You pulled the trigger. What my dad did, what Diane did—yes, it was hurtful, and their actions cannot be justified, but neither one of them made you kill my dad!! Diane did NOT dig my dad's grave. The factors that led to your decision in no way justify your actions and ultimately no one is responsible for my dad's death but you. Were there contributing factors? Sure. But you are the one who ultimately took the situation to a new level and chose to pull that trigger." Words seemed to pour forth like floodwaters as I passionately wrote this rebuke and others into my response.

I held nothing back. I figured if I didn't say these things to him, no one would. I thought perhaps I had been put in this position for that very reason. Perhaps God had placed me in this situation to help Anthony align his thinking with God's and come to a place of repentance.

When I finished my tirade, I reread it with pride in my heart, thinking it was precisely what Anthony needed to hear. I was quite pleased with myself, if you want to know the truth.

I called Sarah right away to read it to her.

"Laurie, that's good," she said when I finished reading. "That is so good!"

"Do you really think so?" I asked, feigning humility while thinking, *I know!* I knew this letter would blow every argument Anthony could possibly make out of the water. I didn't see how he'd be able to get around it.

"Yes!" she said.

"All right. I'm going to send it."

"Do it!" was Sarah's response.

I had every intention of sending this letter. It was a great response that would have put Anthony in his place. But as I held it in my hands, skimming it one last time with prideful arrogance, thinking about how I'd finally be able to give Anthony a piece of my mind, I was reminded of the words God had spoken several weeks before—*You are no better than him.* Immediately, I felt deeply convicted. I knew this was not the response God intended. This letter was not His will. Both Sarah and I had been blinded. Sarah by her desire to protect and defend me— though except for this incident, she has always given sound biblical counsel—and me by my desire to get a little taste of vengeance. I was about to veer off the path God had carved out for me. The path I had so carefully and painstakingly been trying to stay on.

God had called me to love my enemy, not rebuke him. I understood that. But I wondered: *If I don't rebuke him, if I don't set him straight, how will he ever know what he is doing is not okay? How will he be able to see just how twisted his thoughts really are?* Anthony was in prison, sur-rounded by other men who most likely agreed with his line of thinking, as flawed as it was. *How can I allow this man to continue to believe these lies?* I thought. *How can I allow all his blame shifting to go unchecked?* It felt unjust—like I wasn't defending Dad's honor by allowing Anthony's ludicrous thoughts to continue, but it seemed I might have to.

God had made Himself perfectly clear. The letter I had written was not the response He wanted from me, which left me wondering: *If that was not to be my response, how was I to respond?*

This, I did not know.

Chapter 12

FORGIVENESS

I trust God even though He doesn't usually operate on my timeline or do things the way I'd like Him to. I wish I could say that I began trusting God like this the moment I gave my life to Christ, but I didn't. Trust came with time as I saw God work in my life. As I witnessed God's hand begin to work all things for good in my life, I came to believe that God does, in fact, know what He's doing. So when things aren't going my way, I now trust that God must have a better plan—a better way.

I think that's why I decided not to send that letter. I figured God knew something I didn't, and I was pretty sure that God's way would turn out far better than my own.

I was hoping God would tell me what to do quickly, but He didn't. I began praying the moment God told me not to send that letter, but God wasn't answering. So once again, I had to wait, trusting that God would give me direction in His time. I didn't really like to wait for God—I wanted God to answer my prayers right away—but I had learned to be okay with it. I had come to understand that there is purpose in our waiting.

Waiting seems like such a waste of time. But really, it's not. When God makes us wait, He is moving. He is drawing us closer to Himself, showing us that we need Him, molding and shaping our hearts, preparing us in every way for the journey ahead. While we wait, God actively carves out the path He intends for us to take. He goes before us, working in the lives around us, softening hearts to give us favor, fighting unseen battles in the heavens—all so that our path may be unhindered and His will can prevail.

Waiting allows us to demonstrate our trust in God. It is not a waste of time. It is time well spent and an opportunity for us to actively and prayerfully wait on God, who is faithfully working all things according to His good will, for our good and His glory.

So yes, God doesn't usually operate on my timeline, but I'm pretty sure that's a good thing.

My mom came over to my house one day around this time. I think we had planned to go to lunch together with the girls or something, and had decided she'd come over a bit early before we went. The girls were thrilled to see her, as usual yelling, "Grandma!" and running to the door when the doorbell rang.

With hugs and kisses taken care of, Mom asked her usual questions—"How are you? Anything new?"—but I really didn't want to answer. It wasn't the first question I wanted to avoid as much as the second, because I knew that if I were to answer this question honestly—which I would have to do—I would need to talk about Anthony. But I didn't want to.

Mom knew about the correspondence from the beginning and supported it. The day I first told her, she said, "Forgiveness can only be a good thing." I know she meant it, but I still didn't think she really understood why I'd started the correspondence. Since then, we'd talked about how things were progressing with Anthony every now and then, but it had been a while since our last conversation about it. Mom didn't know about all the blame-shifting nonsense or about how things had gotten heated between Anthony and me, and I was hesitant to tell her. That discussion would be emotional, and I wondered if I had the energy for it. Everything was just so complicated and involved.

Mom's questions seemed to linger in the air. I thought it would be nice if I could simply pretend I didn't hear them, but I thought better of it. Mom needed to know what was going on.

"I got another letter from Anthony," I said.

"Oh, you did? When?"

"I don't know. A little while ago."

"What'd he say?"

"Do you want to read it?" I asked.

Mom's interest was piqued. It was the first time I'd offered for her to read a letter.

"Just so you know," I said, "it's not a good letter. You're not going to like it." Mom made an inquisitive expression mixed with a hint of protective anger. I knew her response to what I was doing was about to change—I knew it wouldn't be as favorable as it had been in the past. Mom wasn't going to like that Anthony was getting angry with me. But whatever her response, I knew it would be driven by love. I'm pretty sure I don't know any other person who loves with such an unconditional, selfless, sacrificial love as my mom.

"Why won't I like it?" she asked.

"We're not really in a good place with one another right now," I said carefully. I knew Mom wouldn't like that. She didn't like anyone messing with her kids. "He's justifying what he did and, obviously, that's not okay."

"Honey, I don't know about this—"

"Why don't I just go get the letters," I interrupted. "Hold on."

I walked out of the kitchen and heard Mom say, "Okay," as I headed toward my office.

I thought it would be easier for Mom to read the letters for herself than to have me try to explain them. A moment later, I brought the binder that held both Anthony's and my letters and set it on the kitchen counter before my mom, who sat on one of the barstools.

"You've written this many letters?" she asked.

"Yeah. You can read all of them if you'd like."

"Well, no. I don't have to read them. They're your letters, honey."

"I know, but I don't mind if you read them."

"Are you sure?"

"Yeah. I'm sure. Go ahead." I opened the binder to Anthony's first letter.

Mom began to read as the girls played in the other room and I washed dishes at the same counter she was sitting at. I could tell she was trying to hold back emotion as she read. She still loved Dad and had remained close friends with him after their divorce. His death was just as hard on her as it was on the rest of us. Mom needed healing as much as I did, and so, as she read, I prayed these letters would allow her to see her need to seek God for healing as well.

When she reached the most recent letters, when things began to get more tense between Anthony and me, Mom began to shift in her seat nervously. "Laurie, are you sure you should be doing this? Are you sure this is healthy for you?" she asked.

"Yes, Mom. I'm sure." She continued reading.

"Laurie, he's angry."

"I know, Mom," I said. "Just keep reading."

She did, and when finished, she started in, as I knew she would. "I don't know about this, honey. Anthony's angry. How is this affecting you? Are you doing okay?"

"It's hard," I said, trying to will myself not to cry.

"Yes. It's hard. This has to be hard for you. I'm not sure if this is healthy for you, honey. I don't think you should do this anymore." And that was it—she had hit a nerve. I didn't like her questioning what God was calling me to do. I knew she didn't fully understand what I was doing, but I had hoped she trusted me enough to know that I was doing this because I knew without a doubt that this was God's will.

"Mom," I said curtly, "I know what I am doing. I know this is what God is calling me to do."

"Yeah, but honey, I don't think this is good for you."

"Mom," I said with a little more force, "just because something is hard doesn't mean it's bad for you. I know where God is taking me. I know what He has promised me. I don't know what I'll have to go through to get there, but I know what He told me."

"Where do you think this is going? What good can come out of this?" she asked with concern. "I don't like how this is affecting you."

"I know, Mom, but if God has made one thing clear to me, it is that He is going to bring me to a place of healing and forgiveness. I'm not stopping. God's not done yet."

Mom knew me well enough to know that she wasn't going to get me to budge, so she simply said, "Okay." Even though she didn't agree with what I was doing, I knew I'd still have her support.

Truthfully, I didn't blame Mom for her response. She didn't like this guy messing with her daughter, and in her shoes, I'd try to protect my daughter from trial as well. It's not easy to watch your child willingly step into a fire. But aside from that, Mom was reading letters that were written over time. I had many months to process these letters; she didn't. Reading them all at once must have been like getting doused with a fire hose—I can't imagine the range of emotion she felt. In the end, she was angry. And, quite frankly, I was too. I was still mad at Anthony for making those preposterous statements in his last letter, and I still wanted to rebuke him.

But I wouldn't. That was not God's will.

Weeks later, I was still waiting on God. I did not know how to proceed. After a while, I thought it might be a good idea to get away by myself to clear my head. It isn't often that a stay-at-home mommy to two small girls is able to have some time alone, and I thought if I took a day of fasting and prayer, I might be able to get some clarity on how to proceed.

I decided to go to Lake Tahoe one Saturday, while Travis took the girls somewhere fun to have what we call "special time" with Daddy. It was December. I thought I might still be able to get down to the beach to pray and read my Bible, even though we had already gotten some snow that year. It was worth a shot. I really didn't want to be cooped up inside all day. I wanted to be outside in nature, with God.

It wasn't what I would call a warm day. I knew I would need some layers if I were to be outside, so I packed accordingly, taking nothing but my warmest clothes, my Bible, the binder of letters, and some water. When I got into my car, I filled the silence—usually occupied with children's chatter, laughter, and the occasional tears—with my prayers as I drove the familiar thirty-minute drive up the winding road through the forest to Tahoe.

I grew up in this area, so you might think its sights would be commonplace to me, but they're not. Every time I drop down into the Tahoe basin, I can't help but smile. This is a view I have seen my whole life, but every time I see the lake from this vantage point, I find myself smiling in awe of its magnificence and beauty—and this time was like all the others. As I continued to descend toward the shore, I noticed the snow line was still above lake level. I whispered a prayer of thanks, knowing I'd be able to get down to one of my favorite beaches.

It was cold, and a wind had kicked up by the time I pulled into the parking lot at Burnt Cedar Beach. I was glad I packed the extra layers of clothes. I needed them. Before I got out of the car, I put on every stitch of clothing I'd brought, including a snow hat and cotton gloves that would hopefully keep my hands warm but would be thin enough to turn the pages of my Bible.

Getting out of my car, I threw my warm, fur-trimmed hood over my already beanied head before grabbing my Bible and heading toward the beach. I had planned to sit on the beach itself, but, considering the wind, I thought I might end up with sand in my eyes and decided the grassy peninsula that jets out into the icy blue waters to the beach's right would probably be a better idea.

I was the only person there. No one else dared to brave this wintery day at the beach, and I was glad. I liked having the whole place to myself. I found a bench at the end of the peninsula and sat for quite a while with my face to the wind, praying for clarity—asking God what to do. I opened my Bible and began to read—first in the Psalms, then reading passages at random—before I lay flat, lengthwise on the bench. Closing my eyes, I continued to pray as I lay fully exposed to the elements of God's creation. Fully exposed to God Himself.

God's presence was very real in that place, almost palpable. I had gone to meet with God, and God was most definitely there.

I hated to leave this spot, but I got cold after a few hours and thought it might be a good idea to warm up at the local Starbucks. When I got to the café, I settled in with a nice cup of hot tea—hoping I wasn't breaking any fasting rules. My binder of letters sat on the table in front of me. I had read all the letters before, of course, but never in one sitting, and I thought that if I did so, I might be able to step outside myself and my feelings enough to see things a bit differently.

Sitting there at my little two-top table, I read them all. I had been knee-deep in the trenches for months—focused with my head down and my heart set on winning the battle—but as I read the letters all at once, it was like seeing an aerial view of my battle. I didn't notice anything new, but I did observe everything in a new light. I gained a whole new perspective.

As I read through the letters, at times I felt compassion for Anthony, but when I read the most recent letters once again, I still believed Anthony's claims were beyond ridiculous. Feeling compassion did not change that. I still thought he was wrong and needed to be set straight.

I was trying not to be judgmental, but I didn't think Anthony had ever fully given himself to God. Technically he may have been a Christian—he may have come to trust Jesus for salvation—but I didn't think the gospel had ever really settled in his heart.

I mean, how could it have?

Anthony was justifying—saying he had a "reason" for murdering Dad—when God tells us that there is no justification for murder or any other sin, for that matter. He was blame shifting—saying other people had a part in the murder—when he alone chose to pull that trigger. He was comparing himself and his sentence to others—saying his sentence was not just—when he had committed premeditated murder and had been tried and sentenced under a governing authority that we are to submit ourselves to, according to God.

Almost ten and a half years after he murdered my dad, Anthony still had not taken full responsibility for his actions.

Needless to say, Anthony was far from where I wanted him to be, but after I prayerfully read those letters, God began to work. I went home from the lake to live life as usual, but God never stopped whispering. It seemed He was speaking continually, breaking me of my pride—showing me Scripture after Scripture on forgiveness and love. Once again, I was reminded of the gospel—of the fact that I was far from where God wanted me to be when I was forgiven. Truly, I had been given grace and mercy when I least deserved it.

I wasn't really aware of this all along, but I think I was waiting for Anthony to be where I wanted him to be before I forgave him. I was placing conditions on my forgiveness, but God doesn't do that. He doesn't wait until we've gotten our stuff together before He's willing to forgive us. He doesn't ask us to clean ourselves up before He offers grace. He forgives when we're at our worst—when the depth of our ugliness is revealed. And we're to do the same.

I thought about all of this. And as I did, God said, *Leave him to Me. Now forgive.*

And I did. In the most unlikely moment, God gave me grace to forgive Anthony. For the first time, I knew my forgiveness was real.

In the midst of my anger, when I wanted to rebuke my enemy, God stayed my hand. For weeks had I prayed for God to show me how to proceed, to show me what to do. I had waited on my God, waited for His answer, and it turned out His answer was *grace*.

Grace is what Anthony needed. He didn't need a rebuke. He needed love. For a long time, I thought God wanted to use me to bring Anthony truth, to help him see as he ought to see, but I don't think I was right. Anthony didn't need me to insistently hold him to truth. He needed to be forgiven. He needed love, mercy, and grace—all that God has given me.

Around this time, I wrote, "We do not see eye to eye in many areas, but I've realized it's not my job to make Anthony see as I see, but God's—to help us both see as we ought. All I can do is forgive and be the best ambassador for Christ that I can be to him."

And that was it. I finally got it.

I edited my blog post according to what I knew to be true that same week. My story had changed. It began changing the moment I chose to lay my biases aside and exchange my truth for God's. The only thing that had kept me from editing this post had been pride, and I couldn't keep the post written as it was any longer. So I made some changes and planned to send it with my next letter.

When finished, I revised the letter I had written to Anthony. In his last letter, Anthony had said people call him Tony, not Anthony. I knew that, but I never liked calling him Tony. It was too familiar, too friendly. He was called Anthony in court and in all the media coverage of the murder and, for some reason, I liked that better. I guess it seemed more formal, not so chummy. But if he wanted to be called Tony, I didn't think I should object. So I wrote:

Dear Tony,

I appreciate you writing back despite the fact that my letter upset you. If you choose to discontinue our correspondence I understand, but I'd like to address a few things in your letter first.

Something that I think we both need to keep in mind is that we both have things to say that will upset each other, it's the nature of our relationship, and if we let our pride get in the way, God will not be able to work in our lives to restore and redeem our brokenness.

That being said, I can see how my story has upset you. I will freely admit that there are biases contained within it; however, even though you have given me some of your story, I'm still trying to piece it all together. I truly desire to be able to see the whole situation from an unbiased point of view. Essentially, my goal is to see it as God sees it, not as you see it, not as Diane sees it, not as my dad had seen it, not even as I have seen it in the past, but as God sees it—through the lens of the gospel! I agree that what my dad told me before his murder was biased, I agree that Diane's story is biased, and I know that your story is biased as well. You all have your own perspectives, you all participated in the situation from different points of view, so you all essentially had/have your own "truths," which I am interested in because they each shine a bit more light onto what happened and why. However, I personally believe that none of your "truths" is God's truth. And I pray continually to see it as He does. Frankly, the way I view this tragedy has evolved greatly over the last year, and I praise God for allowing me to get a glimpse into His reality.

After receiving your letter, I went back and read my story, which was written months ago. I did change a few things to better reflect the truths that I believe God has been revealing to me, and I did remove your last name as you requested. With all sincerity, I truly wouldn't want to be the one responsible for shaming or hurting your family.

I recently finished reading this book called *Between a Rock and a Grace Place* by Carol Kent. I believe it's allowed me to see what true repentance looks like (at least from the outside—only God knows one's heart), and it's given me some perspective on our situation as well. It's written by the mother of a man who committed murder, and it's full of his letters to her. His faith and outlook are amazing! It was really helpful for me, and for some reason I feel like it'd help you on your journey as well.

All this being said, if you receive this and you decide to discontinue our correspondence, I understand. I would like you to know, however, that despite the fact that we will probably never see eye to eye in all areas, I do forgive you. Additionally, if you ever feel led to answer my questions, I'd welcome them.

I hope this finds you well, and I pray that God heals you from your past as He is doing for me. I pray that you learn to live your life for God wherever He has you and that you're able to find peace in this life.

Take care, God bless, and have a Merry Christmas.

Sincerely,

Laurie

I sent the letter right before Christmas. It was December 17, 2010, to be exact, seven months after I had first begun corresponding with Anthony. I knew we weren't quite finished yet, but God had already done a mighty work in me, and at the risk of sounding cheesy, I felt free. The burden I had carried with me for over a decade was lifted the moment I forgave. I don't think you ever really know just how heavy a burden you're carrying until it's lifted. And mine was—heavy, that is.

For the first time when I prayed good for Anthony, I actually meant it. I wanted good for him. I wanted to see him come to a good place. I wanted him to find peace in life, even behind bars. I wanted to see him change, to be completely transformed by the gospel. And I wanted to see him come to complete repentance. This wasn't the first time I wanted some of these things, but it was the first time that it wasn't about me. I think I used to want Anthony to be repentant to make myself feel better, but now I wanted these things for him, so he could experience the full blessings of God through a repentant heart.

And so I prayed for change, but I was also content with whatever God's will would be. I thought it would be wonderful if He changed Anthony. But if not, I figured God would have His reasons, and that would be okay too.

I did, however, think the former would make a better story.

Chapter 13

STANDING GROUND

Anthony was pretty upset in his last letter, and I knew he'd thought about quitting on me. So I wasn't sure if he'd write back, but he did. Just over two weeks after I sent my letter, I received Anthony's response:

Dear Laurie,

I received your letter and was thankful that you removed my last name. Thank you. I also admire that fact that you wrote about us working toward forgiveness. It's one thing to do it, it's another thing to announce it to the world.

I wasn't sure you would write me back, but I prayed that God's will would not be stopped by either one of us and that each of us would be opened to the other's understanding of what we are trying to convey. I believe I am trying to convey the truth of what happened, yes, through my eyes, but I am trying not to be biased. I think I am in a unique position to look back objectively because I have had to take responsibly, have been humbled by the selfishness of what I did, and have to live with the consequences every day. I am not trying to clear my name nor trying to put all the blame on someone else. Not all my truths may be God's, but I am trying.

But you also have to be willing to print the truth and the truth is at no time were Rick and Diane "dating." They were having an affair. I know you want to protect your dad and Diane but you cannot white-wash what was going on. In earlier letters you admitted this, why are you minimizing it now? You know God's Word as well as I do. Had they divorced their spouses and married, it would have still been adultery. . . .

And you can say I was enraged if you like, I think that is over dra-matizing it. I was angry and very hurt. But I was trying to cope, I was. I guess it does me no good to explain myself. You seem to believe Diane's side and I understand. But we must be on the same page about this; it was an affair. They never dated. Print that and I promise in my next let-ter to answer all your questions. I will trust you, in that once you've got all your answers, you won't change your story back. I am also going to try to get that book you read. Maybe it will help me too.

Thank you for being patient and for being so open. I am trying to do the same.

God bless.

Anthony

Anthony seemed conflicted to me. I don't know if he really was, but that's what it seemed like. It seemed he was trying to be kind and non-combative at the beginning of this letter and then again at the end, but the middle seemed to take on a different tone altogether. As I read, I felt like Anthony was still trying to go rounds with me. It seemed he still wanted to argue. But I didn't. I was done arguing. I had surrendered my desire to retaliate the moment I forgave him, and no matter what he said to me, I knew God would give me the grace needed to combat his words with love, not anger.

I did not think God was calling me to appease Anthony's every request. Anthony was asking me to do something I wasn't comfortable with. It felt like he wanted me to throw Dad and Diane under the bus, but I wasn't willing to do that. At this time, I didn't think it was my place to write about their relationship. Like I said before, even though

Dad and Diane were clearly engaged in an inappropriate relationship in the eyes of God, no one really knew the particulars of that relationship, and if I succumbed to Anthony's request it would only cause Diane more pain. I certainly didn't want to do that.

If I were to write about this portion of the story on my blog, it would be misunderstood. It was all so complicated, and you can't give adequate context to a complicated situation in one paragraph of a four-hundred- to seven-hundred-word blog post. It's just not possible. To this day, I refuse to write about the causes behind the murder in article format for that very reason. There's simply not enough room to give the adequate details needed to understand what really went on. And, quite frankly, telling what went on between Dad and Diane lends very little to the story God has given me to share. My story isn't about adultery. In a way, it's not even about murder. It's about redemption.

Anthony seemed to be holding the answers to my questions over my head to get what he wanted, but I wasn't willing to do anything God wasn't calling me to do for the sake of getting answers. Don't get me wrong. I wanted the answers. I was desperate to know what Anthony knew. I wanted to know what went on in that house the day of the murder. I wanted to know what Dad's last moments were like—if he was scared, if he knew he was going to die, if he said something before he died, if he died quickly, if he was in pain. These questions had plagued me from the moment I was told of Dad's death. I had spent more than a decade wondering what that terrible night must have been like for Dad. But I wasn't willing to compromise my integrity for the answers.

I felt like Anthony's request was a test to see just what I would do to get what I wanted. And it was tempting—let me tell you, it was super tempting—but I just couldn't do it.

I thought and prayed about this decision for two weeks before I finally wrote back:

Dear Tony,

I apologize for taking so long to write back. I've had to do a lot of thinking and praying about what you said in your last letter.

I do agree with you about printing the truth. I've thought a lot about what you said, and while I've tried to protect my dad and Diane up to this point, I agree that if I expose the details of your sins then I must be willing to do the same with all those involved, my dad and Diane included. Yet whenever I thought about doing this, I had a constant feeling of uneasiness. . . .

Additionally, when I received your last letter, all that kept going through my mind was the fact that I only wanted to do what was right in the sight of God. Despite my desire to have answers to my questions, in no way would I ever compromise my integrity or my morals in order to get answers. That's why it's taken so long to write you back. Essentially, the only reason I would make any changes would be on the basis of doing the right thing. The right thing by my dad, by Diane, by you . . . and most especially by God.

Consequently, I've decided to omit the details of the murder completely in my post. My post still has the details of what happened that directly affected me, but I've edited out the two paragraphs describing what led up to the murder. I may, in the future, decide to write more about the details, but only if or when I feel God's leading me to do so, and only if it's the right thing to do. If I ever do write about the details, I feel convicted to write the whole truth about all parties. However, at this time, I'm feeling like it's not my place to expose the sins of others. We'll see where God leads me.

Anyway, if you feel led to give me answers, then please do so. If not, I understand.

I hope this finds you well. I pray that you find the peace and forgiveness you're looking for. Getting that book I recommended may help in this quest. If I can be of help as well, let me know.

Take care and God bless,

Laurie

When I finished writing, I said a little prayer, asking God to lay it upon Anthony's heart to answer my questions only if it was in His will for Anthony to do so. I still wanted the answers, but in that moment I stopped striving for them. I laid my request before God and figured it was in His hands.

I wanted Anthony to experience forgiveness for himself. I wanted him to be set free as I had been. His last few letters seemed to reveal a lot of resentment and pain, and I knew that if Anthony didn't seek God to forgive, he would never experience the fullness of God. He would never experience the love and joy and peace God offers to each of us through Christ. But it didn't have to be like that.

Despite his appeal, Anthony would most likely spend the rest of his life in prison for what he had done to my dad, but that didn't mean he had to waste whatever time he had left. What if he could bring life while in there? I had a vision in my mind of what God could do through this man, if only he came to a right, fully repentant, fully redeemed relationship with Jesus. I knew that if this man changed through the power of God, others would be healed as well. Others would come to know and love and serve our mighty God. God could use Anthony to transform lives—many lives. But first, he needed healing; he needed to forgive.

And so I thought perhaps I might be able to help him do so.

Chapter 14

HEARTS SOFTENED

It was January. Winter had settled in. A soft blanket of snow covered the ground a few inches thick, giving the girls the opportunity to put on their snow gear to play and build a snowman, complete with hat and scarf. The temperatures ranged from the high teens to mid twenties, which was nothing out of the ordinary for this time of year, but that didn't stop me from walking a block through the snow with my girls to the mailbox each day to see if Anthony had written.

Of course, I'd be lying if I told you it had nothing to do with the answers, but that wasn't the only reason I was waiting for this next letter with an extra measure of expectancy. You see, I didn't think God was finished yet. He had already done a mighty work in me, and I couldn't help but think He was about to do something big in Anthony as well.

My mind was filled with imaginings of what God might do—truthfully, I could hardly wait to see how God would play our crazy story out—so I began to wait for and welcome Anthony's letters with joyful anticipation like never before. It was a far cry from the days, not so long before, when even the sight of one of these letters turned my stomach and brought tears to my eyes.

The letter came one week after I sent mine. I was glad Anthony wrote quickly this time. After bringing the letter into the house, I found myself standing in my kitchen once again, opening the familiar envelope. I think I was a bit too excited to sit, so I continued to stand there. The girls danced around me in oblivion, as I read:

Dear Laurie,

I got your letter and wanted to write you back quickly. I lost your list of questions that you'd like answered. I had them but we get "shookdown" (searches) and they aren't neat about it. The list must have gotten thrown out. Please send me a new one and I will do my best to answer them all.

Also any insights you had from your dad would be appreciated, even if they hurt. Plus some advice, how do I put myself in Diane's shoes and understand, what to me, is un-understandable? I'm not saying I would have never had an affair. I think under the "wrong" circumstances anyone is susceptible. But I would have never torn my family apart for anyone. The fact is I loved Diane, I wish I had loved her the way she wanted, but I guess I didn't.

. . . Now that I ask you to print, what we both know to be the truth you've changed your story a third time. [But] I think what you've written now is what I'd wish you'd written in the first place. And not because of what you've taken out, but what you've added! You have made it focussed on you and God. It is a true and very touching testimony. I also was taught by my pastor that forgiveness is not about them but on you and how God frees those who chose to forgive. Sometimes it's like they say in AA, a minute by minute decision. When some of the old anger or hurt I feel pops up, I catch it and pray to God, "Help me Lord to forgive again." And as His word says, He is faithful. Laurie, this was a truly inspiring testimony, and though it may mean nothing to you, I am proud of you for posting it.

I have felt, through much prayer, that you deserve to know what happened, send me your questions, and I will answer. But, even though I've been writing that letter in my head for some time and would much rather tell you in person, be patient. It may take a couple (or more) weeks to write it. Thank you for your letter and testimony. I won't keep the letter, but I want to keep the testimony, is that OK?

Sincerely and God bless,

Anthony

I smiled and whispered a prayer of thanks as I read this letter. God was moving. He was answering my prayers. I had started to think Anthony would never tell me what happened the day Dad died, but it sounded like I was going to get my answers after all. Even greater was that, as I read this letter, I couldn't help but think God was beginning to change Anthony. He seemed humbler, somehow. There was a softness I had never seen before. All contention seemed to have vanished.

God's grace is a beautiful thing. It's intended to trickle down, and that's precisely what it was doing. Anthony was asking me to help him do the very thing I had just done. To understand the "un-understandable." To forgive the seemingly unforgivable. And though I didn't realize it at the time, it took a lot of humility for Anthony to allow the daughter of the man he murdered—the man who, in his eyes, took his wife—to speak into his life. Since this time, I've come to see that I was just as much Anthony's enemy as he was mine, and, in this moment, he humbled himself enough to ask his enemy for help.

God was beginning to create beauty out of ashes—just as He promises. Scripture was being played out in my life's story, and I just couldn't seem to get over the beauty of what God was doing right before my eyes. The thought of God using me to help bring forgiveness and healing to the very one who had harmed me was a beautiful thing. I saw it as a picture of the gospel itself.

Two days later, I sat down and wrote my response. I figured the quicker I wrote back, the quicker I'd finally be able to know what had happened that terrible day. It was a novel of a letter. Anthony had asked to know what I knew, and apparently I had a lot to say on that topic:

Dear Tony,

Thank you for writing so quickly. I thought I'd try to keep that ball rolling as well, but I understand that it'll probably take you a while to write back to this, and that's okay. Just for the record, I don't mind you keeping any of our correspondence as long as you agree not to use it to further your appeal (I think we already established that).

As far as my blog posts go, I do understand that it might seem like I keep changing my story, giving you the feeling that I might have an agenda of sorts, but I assure you that's not the case. The only agenda I have is to seek out God's truth in this whole mess. One thing that you need to understand is that my story has been changing, or a better word for it I think would be evolving, over time as a result of what I believe to be God's truth shedding more light on our situation. As mentioned before, I pray unceasingly to see this situation through the lens of the gospel and, consequently, the way I view it has definitely changed over time. I think we all have this evolution of the way we view our past. This was happening on its own to me (in regards to my dad's death) over the last ten years, but it wasn't until the last year and a half, when I really began to seek God in this, that I really started viewing the situation, and consequently you, drastically differently. I believe God has been revealing His truth to me.

I never started out with the intention to favor one party over another, but I now know that's precisely what I ended up doing initially. You were the bad guy in my mind, and so I spoke the truth (my truth) that I had at the time. . . . Through much prayer, however, God began to show me that sin is sin. You all sinned against our holy God, as do we all minute to minute, and there are consequences to our sins. I was talking to my pastor about it a while ago, and he reminded me that the penalty for all sin is death, so you all essentially deserved the penalty of death. Currently, however, I believe you all equally had a hand in what took place. This doesn't mean that I think you should not face your consequences. My dad certainly had to face his. . . . It is only through the grace of God that you all are still able to be forgiven of your sins through the person and work of Jesus. This obviously doesn't just apply to you guys, it's true for all who place their trust in Jesus as you well know. Additionally, I think it's VERY important to take full responsibility for each of your own actions and not blame-shift.

. . . You asked how you might be able to put yourself in Diane's shoes. Well, I'd begin by praying, as I'm sure you're already doing. Pray to see the whole situation through God's eyes—to see God's truth. Pray for the ability to see it through Diane's eyes (though this, of course, would be a biased point of view just as yours and my dad's would be but it's important and helps to go there). Pray that He will someday soften Diane's heart toward reconciliation and communication with you.

. . . Try to place yourself in her shoes. From my point of view, divorce/separation isn't only the fault of the one initiating or committing the actions—two people are in a marriage, and it take two people to destroy a marriage. All of these same questions can be asked of Diane as well. Try to see your marriage from her side. What was it like being married to you? How did you talk to her, how did you treat her . . . were you kind/loving or harsh/irritable/unloving? How did your actions affect her throughout your marriage? What was it like to have you be the father of her child? Reflect back on your memories, and try to envision those memories from where she was standing in them. Frankly, nothing comes out of nowhere, so what, in her perspective [led] to her straying and being unhappy in the marriage? With the building of the house, what was it like for her? What did she experience? Why might she and my dad have gotten close? As far as the period during the separation/divorce, what might she have been going through? . . . As far as the murder, how did this affect Diane? What might her experiences have been throughout the events leading up to and during and after the murder? How have your actions affected the way she currently views you? If you were her, and she murdered the woman you were in a relationship with, how might you currently view her? Would you be angry with her?

Would you feel guilty? How would her actions affect you? How would these actions impact your life? . . . Would you still fear her, considering her previous lack of adherence to the law/lack of self-control? What if she got out of prison, would you be scared, especially if you didn't know whether or not she had a repentant heart? Would you consider her to be a mentally stable person, if the tables were turned?

All of these questions and many more could help you to put yourself in her shoes in the past and even now, and once you're able to do this, you can then begin to understand, which could lead to forgiveness. We are all products of our environments. We are all affected by those around us and what we go through in our life—looking at another's life situations is very helpful to see why the person is the way they are.

As far as my dad's perspective: As I think I mentioned to you before, my dad only talked to me about the situation two or three times. I was in college, so I was removed from the situation as well. Remember, this was the point of view of my dad. I'm sure it was/is biased. Where or how he came to these conclusions is unknown. Some of this may be hard to hear, but just as I've endured some of the difficult things you've had to say, try to maintain an open mind.

What I know: My dad told me that he built you and Diane a house, that your marriage was on the rocks during construction, that you were often not very nice, and that you were an unkind husband. Essentially, my dad was under the impression that you were abusive, mostly verbally, but also physically, to Diane. His impression of you was that you were not a good guy. The impression that I got was that he was essentially trying to "save" Diane from an abusive relationship. My dad was the kind of guy who likes to "rescue," in a sense, those in need. Apparently, he thought you were a "loose cannon," that you were mentally unstable. He told me about the threat to commit suicide. He told me he and Diane mostly had a relationship over the phone because they wanted to be careful due to the fact that you and Diane were negotiating custody, and she wanted it to be favorable for her. He alluded to me (though only

Diane, my dad, and God know the truth) that [they] weren't sleeping together, but that he did love her.

You questioned in a previous letter why would someone stay together with a woman he didn't know very well if he felt that his life was being threatened (which I believe he did). I personally disagree with your assessment in this area. My dad was the type of guy who would risk himself for those he loved. He loved Diane. I saw it in his eyes when he talked about her. I know that may be hard to hear. But he was madly in love with her. He wanted to marry her, and I believe they would have gotten married had he not been killed.

One blessing that came from their relationship is that Diane actually led my dad to Christ! My dad grew up Catholic. He and my mom took us to the Catholic church growing up (which I completely turned away from at the age of fifteen), but though they both always believed in God, they never had a relationship with Jesus. This all changed during my dad's relationship with Diane. He began talking to me about his new-found faith, which I dismissed quickly because I was an agnostic at the time. Frankly, though it is crazy, God used their relationship to bring my dad to Himself! God always promises that he will bring blessings out of our sufferings, and this is one of those blessings.

A little about my dad's life . . . He and my mom met young and got married when they were nineteen. They had my brother when twenty-one, my sister when twenty-three, and me when twenty-five. They were so young, and they had a good marriage for twenty-two years. Then my dad's dad died when he was sixty-three (my dad was around forty at the time), and I think my dad started to see the brevity of life. He went through a crisis of his own and soon left my mom. After dating, he met [a woman] and got married. He soon discovered that he wasn't happy and that's when Diane came into the picture.

I tell you all of this because I think it helps to know one's background to understand him or her. To see him for who he was, what he went through, etc. My dad was an amazing dad. He was always there for us, and before my parents' divorce, we were always going fishing, camping, hiking, hunting, water/snow skiing and much, much more. I was definitely a "daddy's girl," but there was a period of time during and after my parents' divorce that our relationship was strained because I was very mad at him for leaving my mom. Fortunately, we were able to repair our relationship before his death, and we were close again. The last five or six years of his life were difficult for him. This was the time after his dad died, and he sort of fell apart. As mentioned, he left my mom after twenty-two years of marriage and began looking for something to fix himself, something to make him happy, etc. It was during this period of his life that he was not acting like himself. Prior to this, he was an upstanding, kind, loving, happy family man. But life has a way of changing things. Additionally, what he was searching for, the only thing that can make us happy, he wasn't able to find until the last six to twelve months in his life—a relationship with our Savior. It's tragic and ironic that the relationship which helped lead him to Christ was the same relationship that led to his demise and his death.

Okay, enough of that. Let me know if you have any questions about the information I gave you, and I'd be happy to clarify. I hope that the above helps you in your path toward peace and forgiveness.

On to my questions . . . this is what I originally wrote:

"As you know, I attended your trial every day, so I know what was said there. What I would like to ask you, though, is for your story. Much light was shed on this topic during the trial, but I'd like to have your perspective. How did this happen? Why did this happen? What led you to this point? What really went on in my dad's house on August 5th? What was the tone of your conversation? What was said (on my dad's part as well as yours)? What set you off? Did my dad say something before you shot him? What were my dad's last words? Also, were you truly a Christian at this time or were you just going through the motions? Where are you at now as far as your faith goes? I'm not asking for you to justify what you did because what you did can never be justified, and it will never be okay. But I do realize that you have insight into the situation that I have yet to hear. As much detail as you can provide would be much appreciated."

I know some of these have been answered, such as the questions about your faith. Basically, though, I'd like to know what you know—everything that you know, especially about what happened that day. Please tell me everything that happened and, if you're able to, tell me what was going through your mind at the time as well. I'm sure you've gathered that I don't buy the story told in court. I don't believe that the gun just went off accidentally, so what really did happen? I understand you wanted to scare him—did it work? Was he scared? Did you tell him you were going to kill him? If so, what was his response? What did you talk about? What were his last words? Thank you for your honesty and the willingness to answer my questions! I know it won't be easy to hear, nor will it be easy to write, but I do feel as though I need to know the truth.

I pray that all those involved—you, Diane, your son, my mom, my brother and sister, my grandparents, my aunts and uncles, my cousins, your parents, and the rest of your family—can get to a place of peace and forgiveness! The effect of this situation spread far and wide, perhaps our interactions will be the beginning of healing for all those affected!

I pray for God's will in your life, and that He uses you where you are for His purposes to further the gospel! Be an ambassador right where you are! Be sure not to waste your life in there. I believe we're all placed right where we're supposed to be. I was listening to a sermon by John Piper the other day. What was so prominent about this particular sermon was his call for all God's children to not waste their lives. Most of us do, and that's a tragedy. Just because you're in prison, doesn't mean that you've wasted your life. Allow the Spirit of God to use you in there to transform lives according to His will!!! Do not let my dad's death be in vain. Do not let your life be in vain. God wants to use you!

I hope you are well.

Take care and God bless,

Laurie

Anthony's next letter couldn't come fast enough. He had told me to be patient, and I was trying, but I could hardly wait to get my hands on that next letter. I was so close to finally being able to know what had really happened to my dad. Weeks before, I had put my desire for answers in God's hands—and I really had stopped striving for those answers for a little while—but now that I knew they were coming, I found it ridiculously difficult to continue to wait with patience. All I wanted was to know.

Several days after I sent my letter, I found myself once again braving wintery conditions to check my mailbox day after day, hoping I'd see that familiar envelope lying in the pile of that day's mail. Anthony had told me not to expect his response for at least two weeks, but being a hopeful optimist, I thought he might finish sooner than he had originally thought, so I continued to check.

Ten days after I sent my last letter to Anthony, I peered into that mailbox as I had so many times before, but this day, I saw what I had been waiting for. I think my heart might have skipped a beat when I saw the letter's edge poking out from underneath all the other envelopes. My answers were finally here, and I just about leapt for joy. I'm pretty sure if it hadn't been so cold outside, I'd have opened that letter right there on that icy sidewalk, but as it was, I figured the girls and I ought to get inside where it was warm.

After getting home, I set the girls up with an activity, thinking I'd have to spend some time with this letter, and began to read:

Dear Laurie,

I got your letter and wanted to acknowledge it. I will begin on the letter you've been asking for.

I want to read your story to our church. I think it can have a powerful impact upon the men here. I will tell them this is what God can do in their lives if they place Him in the middle of a relationship. He can truly work miracles.

I'd like to finish it by reading the last paragraph you wrote me in the last letter. For you to encourage me in such a way, for me, is truly inspiring. It and this whole process has placed in my heart a very vivid and real picture of what forgiveness is, and it has also moved me to a place where I want forgiveness in all areas of my life. . . .

I understand how your story has been evolving, and I believe I even said you didn't need the stuff about me. And I think it is more powerful without it. I have tried to look at myself from Diane's perspective and answer your questions. . . . I thought I was doing what I was supposed to be doing, working, providing, cleaning, but there is more to it than that, and I learned that lesson too late.

And if I ever get out, nobody needs to fear me. My heart is repentant, and I only want to live in peace.

. . . If your dad thought there was physical abuse in my marriage, he was mistaken or misled. I never touched Diane in anger till the day your dad and I got into our fight. I could line up everyone in our church, back then, and they would all have told you I was a good guy. I dealt with your dad during construction, remember I plumbed the house myself, and never had a cross word with him. . . . You have to also remember maybe your dad was trying to make it seem OK what he was doing. Kind of justifying it in his mind. He wasn't saving her, he was taking her. Maybe he wanted to think he was rescuing her, but I think he knew better. As for him being in love with her, I will take your word on that. You knew him, and if you saw it in his eyes, then I wouldn't dispute it.

And as for Diane leading him to Christ, I say thank God! I have worried over that for years, wondering if I sent someone to hell before he had an opportunity to accept Christ as his Lord and Savior. I don't deserve to have my burden or guilt lightened, but knowing this does. It does give me a little peace, thank you for telling me. I use to think badly of your dad, think he was the bad guy. I no longer feel that. We all, Diane, myself, and your dad behaved wrongly. We did things I'm sure we wish we could take back if we could. But I inflicted the most pain and horror. For that I am truly sorry for everything to everyone.

I am humbled by your forgiveness and uplifted by your encouragement. I will try to live my life for God and not allow your dad's life to
have been in vain, nor mine. I will begin writing your next letter and
thank you for your insights, your admonishments, your honesty, and
forgiveness.

God bless,

Anthony

Thank You, I whispered to Jesus when I finished reading. Tears rolled
down my cheeks as I closed my eyes and simply sat in God's over-
whelming grace and presence. This was not the letter I had hoped for,
but it did not disappoint.

For quite some time, I had worried that if I wasn't insistent upon
truth, Anthony would never come to it, but I was mistaken. Anthony's
heart was changing—he was being transformed by the renewal of his
mind, as Scripture says—right before my eyes. This was clearly not my
doing, but God's. All the blame shifting and justifying had stopped,
not because of any lofty argument made by me, but because God was
at work.

Chapter 15

THE LONG-AWAITED LETTER

I had always longed to be with my dad during his last moments on earth. I've never really told anyone that before, but it's true. I wanted to be there at his deathbed. I wanted to tell him that I loved him—that he was the best daddy I could have ever hoped for. I wanted to hear him tell me whatever it was he would have told me before he died. I wanted to sit by his side and hold his hand as he took his last breath. And I wanted to hear his last words.

I wanted *these* moments with Dad.

I wanted to be there, but I wasn't.

Anthony was.

He took these moments from me, and even though I no longer held resentment toward Anthony for all he had done, I still felt like he had something that belonged to me. He had memories of Dad's last moments that no one else had. I thought that maybe if I could just know all there was to know about the moments I missed, then perhaps I'd receive, in some small part, what should have been mine in the first place. Giving me answers might just return a small portion of what had been stolen.

But it wasn't going to be easy for Anthony to write that letter. I knew that. It would be hard for him to unearth that day. I'm sure he'd much rather keep it all neatly buried. But I also knew God was calling him into that dark pit to release the demons of his past. Anthony was listening, and for that, I was thankful.

Anthony told me he wasn't sure if these answers would bring me the peace I hoped they would. I wasn't sure if he was right or not, but I figured they couldn't hurt me any more than I had already been hurt. And whatever Anthony had to say in this letter would be met with grace, not condemnation. The forgiveness God had worked in my heart was complete. It was unconditional, and I knew in the depths of my soul that nothing would be able to take that away.

I was growing more anxious to receive Anthony's next letter with each passing day. The last one—as good as it was—had me fooled a bit. I was all geared up to receive my answers, and I thought they had come with that letter. But they hadn't. I had been waiting and watching for my answers like a little girl anxiously awaits the arrival of her grandparents, saying, "They're here!" each time headlights approach, only to watch disappointed as one set of headlights after another passes by.

Ever since Anthony wrote, "Print that and I promise in my next letter to answer all your questions," I had hoped each letter would be *the* letter. But with two letters and well over a month gone by, I was finding it increasingly difficult to wait. Knowing that I would get to know what had happened intensified my desire exponentially, and so once again I found myself checking the mail every afternoon in the cold of winter, hoping I'd receive that much-coveted letter.

I checked that mailbox day after day for what seemed like an eternity before the letter finally came—only seven days after the previous letter's arrival. Pulling it out of the mail pile, I clutched that letter close to my heart as I hurried back to the house.

I stood in my kitchen, holding this letter with one hand on each side, as if it were some sort of prized possession, and whispered, "Lord, help me," as I nervously flipped it over and opened the envelope. I fully expected this letter to be like all the others, but when I pulled out its contents, I found not one but two letters, folded separately, in the same envelope.

Dear Laurie,

Well I guess this is the letter you're been waiting a year for. I wish we could do this face to face.

But first some amazing news. I read your testimony at our church service yesterday and today. I told them what an amazing God we serve that could bring two people at opposite ends of the spectrum together in forgiveness. That this story has particular meaning to me cuz I'm who it was written about, I'm the one who killed her dad. I then said not only had you forgiven me, but you'd encouraged me. Then I read the last paragraph of your last letter! I told them nothing is unforgivable, Christ was crucified for every sin. I told them to place God in the center of their most broken relationship and pray. They may not find that kind of forgiveness, but they would find forgiveness in them, and then they'd know the peace that surpasses all understanding.

There were men crying, one guy stood up and said he'd lost his wife to another man (I didn't tell them why I had done what I'd done). He said for the last few months he had decided when he got out he was going to kill the man. Now he'd decided to pray and forgive. Your testimony may have saved a life! How awesome is our God! God has used you and me and this horrible crime to heal, not only us, but others. Now your forgiveness has truly settled into my heart. I won't let your dad's life nor mine be in vain, I promise. Thank you for making it possible to share this amazing testimony. I believe God is not finished with either of us, tomorrow is a good day.

Thank you,

Anthony

I was stunned, completely overwhelmed with emotion. Tears fell from my eyes. I stood, simply staring at this letter in silent disbelief.

I couldn't believe what God had done. I mean I knew it was true, but it was just so amazing. *Oh Lord*, I thought, as I closed my eyes and dropped my head back in awe. "You are so good," I said aloud, "Thank You, Jesus. Thank You."

I was overtaken. God had been redeeming what seemed unredeemable right before my very eyes—bringing good out of evil to an extent I could not have imagined. I had seen hints of this all along. I knew God was beginning to redeem this terrible tragedy the moment I set out on this path. When I began this whole thing, I knew God would redeem my past. I knew He would bring me the healing I needed, and I even thought He might redeem Anthony as well, but even though I had a strong sense that God was on the move, I didn't think He'd take it this far.

A memory flashed through my mind of the day I sat at the park after Dad's funeral. I remembered wrestling through pain and anger, questioning, "How could there be a reason for this?" Dad's murder had seemed so meaningless. I didn't think any good could come out of it. But as I read that letter and saw God use Dad's death for good, I found its purpose. And in that moment, I felt Jesus whisper to my heart, *This is what your journey is about, Laurie. It's not about your past. But what I will do with your past if you continue to follow Me wherever I may lead.*

And at once, I understood.

In his letter to the church in Philippi, Paul wrote, "But one thing I do: forgetting what lies behind and straining forward to what lies ahead, I press on toward the goal for the prize of the upward call of God in Christ Jesus" (Phil. 3:13–14).

"Forgetting what lies behind."

"Straining forward to what lies ahead."

"I press on."

It wasn't about my past. It was about my future. About how God might use me and my story of redemption to bring light and hope to others. To show that absolutely nothing is unredeemable through Jesus. Nothing.

Nine months before this, I had begun to pray for Anthony out of simple obedience to God's call to love my enemy. Jesus tells us, "Love your enemies and pray for those who persecute you" (Matt. 5:44), and so I did. It was contrary to everything I was feeling at that time, but I prayed that Anthony would receive that which was good. I prayed God would change him. I prayed God would heal him. I prayed God would bring him to complete repentance. And I even prayed Anthony would be used to the glory of God in prison. It was a pipe-dream prayer, I thought. I knew God could do it but, quite honestly, I didn't think He would. Then He did. God answered my prayers—every one of them.

"I prayed for this," I said aloud. No one was in the room with me, but I think I had to say it to believe it.

Wiping the tears from my eyes, I looked at the second letter I had pulled out of the envelope. It was three pages long, front and back, and it contained all I ever wanted to know. It was the letter I had been anxiously waiting for, but after reading that first letter, it didn't seem to matter as much anymore. I still wanted to know what had happened that terrible day, but it didn't hold the same weight it once did.

With all sense of urgency gone, I walked over to my couch and settled in to read the letter I had always wanted to read*:

Dear Laurie,

O.K. I'm not sure how to approach this, and I don't want to hurt you. I also don't remember everything that was said, but I will try to do the best I can.

---

*Anthony had entrusted the truth to me with this letter, and I have always wanted to honor that. Anthony asked me to keep some of the details he shared to myself, but he gave me permission to talk about this letter with those I trust. I have kept that promise to this day.

When writing this book, I went through this letter line by line with Anthony over the phone, asking for permission to include what I have. We both wanted to include as much of this letter as possible but chose to omit only the sections that could cause further pain to those involved.

That morning, I had a friend and her two sons over. I was going to fix the stereo in her truck when the police pulled up to arrest me. As you know, I had driven on Carson River Road, which came within 100 yards of our house. On the way to the jail the officer told me Diane must really want me arrested because he had gone out there the night before and told her I was too far away. But she had called him back that morning because her friend, your dad, had measured it, and it fell within the 100 yards. He told me this as we drove past your dad's house. I was very upset because the D.A. said she'd put me in jail for six months, and I wouldn't see [my son]. I had given up on Diane, but not seeing [my son] was killing me. The thought of not seeing him for six months drove most rational thought from my head.

I began to focus on your dad while I was waiting to bail out. . . . So when I got out, I walked home with the intent to drive over to your dad's house and tell him to stay away from [my son] while I was gone. I took my gun to scare him into believing I meant it. After the fact, my attorney told me I couldn't say that because that's why they charged me the way they did. If I wanted to scare him, I'd be admitting to intent to assault or batter.

. . . So I drove over. His garage was open, so I went to the door and knocked. He answered and jumped. I did have the gun pointed at him. He backed up and then got down on his knees. I told him I just wanted to talk, to get up. He backed up and stood by the table. I told him I wanted him to stay away from [my son] while I was in jail. He told me it was never his intent to get between me and my son, that he had a son too.

I think he was still there when he told me he was going to move to Wyoming. I said, "You're moving?" He said yes, he had a "spread" up there. I asked him if he intended to take Diane. He said no. He wanted to get away from it all. Then he turned and started to walk away. I had not had the gun pointed at him during this conversation, but as he walked away he was heading for the hall. I pointed the gun at him and repeated I only wanted to talk. He changed course and went to his sofa and sat. I got down on my knees and rested the gun over the back of the other love seat. I didn't have any [sub-conscious] motives, I just didn't want to go into his living room.

So I remember he picked up a hunting magazine and said if I wanted to continue being able to hunt I should leave. I said I would eventually. Somehow the conversation turned to the day in December when we fought. . . . It was hot in there, and I wanted to leave. . . .

[Things were said.] I pulled the trigger. I don't know if I expected the gun to fire. I don't remember aiming it. I don't remember even chambering a round, but it went off and your dad fell over.

. . . I went to get up and as I testified, I caught the clip on the couch, and the gun fired again. I don't or didn't know where he'd been hit. I started to run out. When I got to the garage door, I thought I needed to check on him, so I turned around and walked back, calling his name. As I peeked around the corner, I saw all the blood coming out of his ear. I panicked and ran. I must have closed the garage door as I ran past.

That's what happened. I'm so sorry I wish I could take it all back.

. . . I told my attorney it was accidental. . . . I wasn't going to tell people what really happened anyway. I'd go down, and I knew it. You are the only one besides my appeal attorney who knows, and he's not telling anyone either. I pray you will keep it to yourself and those in your family you trust.

I'm sure you'll have questions, so take your time, and if you do, I'll answer them. I know this hurt Laurie, but I also hope it helped you in the ways you'd hoped for.

Sincerely,

Anthony

Anthony was telling the truth for the very first time, telling me things he hadn't told anybody else. He told me what happened moment by moment from the time he came to Dad's house until he left. He told me what was said—both by him and by Dad, to the best of his recollection, and I knew he was being honest. I could practically hear Dad's voice in my head as I read some of what Anthony quoted him saying. It was sad, hearing that distant echo of Dad's voice through Anthony's letter, but it provided an odd comfort as well. The sound of Dad's voice had grown quiet over the years, and I missed it, so in a weird way, it was nice to have it brought to mind again, even though the context was not good.

The murder wasn't an accident, as Anthony claimed in his defense. The gun didn't just "go off"—Anthony had pulled that trigger intentionally. I had always known that, but I was glad to finally see Anthony admit it. There was no more dancing around the truth. It was all out in the open, and even though the truth hurt—even though this letter was hard for me to read—it did bring closure, as I had hoped it would. I finally knew what I wanted to know.

Peace settled in my heart for the first time since Dad had died. I was finally at peace with my past—with all that had happened. But I don't think peace came because of the answers alone. It was more than that. With that first letter, God had shown me that it wasn't about my past but about how He would use my past to help others. There was peace in knowing that all I had been through wasn't for naught. In knowing that there was purpose in my pain. That nothing would be wasted. It would all be used to bring good to this world. To bring hope to many and glory to God.

Life was busy at this time. Travis and I had begun the process of adopting from Ethiopia several months before and were in the thick of all sorts of paperwork. We were running around like crazy, getting documents in order, with little time to spare. I wanted to respond to Anthony right away, but I didn't want to rush my response. I had so much I wanted to say, and I wanted to ensure I said it well. So ten days passed before I was finally able to carve out enough time to sit down and respond appropriately:

Dear Anthony,

I am so sorry it's taken me so long to get back to you! Especially in light of your last two letters. Life has been very busy lately for me. Travis, my husband, and I are in the process of adopting one/two babies from Ethiopia, and I've been working on applications for grants, which all have deadlines for their submission. It's been consuming all of my spare time lately!

Anyway, first of all, I have to address the first letter in your last mailing regarding the reading of my testimony in your church. Frankly, I'm at a loss! I'm amazed and humbled, though not surprised, that God has used us in this way. When I began this journey toward forgiveness and when I first contacted you, for whatever reason, I knew God was going to do something big through this situation. And I agree, for whatever reason, I think this is only the beginning of God using our past tragedies for His Glory and for His purposes. Thank you for allowing God to use you! I know that if you and I continue to follow His lead, to keep close to Him, to put Him at the center of our lives and our relationships, amazing things will happen, to the glory of God!!

Additionally, after reading through your two last letters, I can just see God's grace upon our situation. He is so unbelievably true to His promises, and our situation is such an example of what God can do when you place Him at your center!!

In fact, just as He's changed both of our hearts throughout our communication, and He seems to be changing hearts through our testimony there in prison, He's changing hearts out here as well with the testimony of our correspondence . . . but the bottom line is that we can be used by God and make a real impact for Him and His Kingdom!!

. . . As you said, my dad could have been justifying his actions by feeling like he was "rescuing" Diane. I truly don't know.

On to your last letter—It was difficult to hear, but I thank you for answering my questions. I did need to hear it, and though the details didn't evoke a sense of peace, it did give me peace to know more about what my dad's last moments were like, thanks be to God!!

. . . One last thing. I'd like to ask for your forgiveness as well for all the anger, bitterness, and resentment I held against you for such a long time, and for thinking of you more as a murderer than a person. Also for any offense I've committed against you, throughout our communication and for the last ten years. It's not as if I spent the last ten years thinking/talking about you, but on rare occasion, if it were to come up, I definitely didn't have your interest in mind. You were my dad's murderer. The bad/evil guy. But you are a child of God, and you deserve to be treated with dignity.

I hope this finds you well! Keep living for God in there. I truly believe God has you there for His purposes!!

God bless,

Laurie

That week, I wrote an e-mail to Pastor Bobby as well, telling him what God had done:

I have to say, I'm just amazed at the goodness and grace of God in this situation! Throughout this difficult process of communication/forgiveness/healing, I've sought God's will, and He has been so faithful to not only carry me through, but to guide me, to comfort me, to heal me, and the list goes on! Additionally, I've witnessed not only the transformation of my heart, but Anthony's as well. Reading through his letters, you can just see and hear God's transformative powers! Not only that, but He's using my dad's murder for good! It's all Him! None of it has been me. How great is our God! I've just obeyed. I know He's not even close to being done using this tragedy for His glory. I get the sense that this is only the beginning. . . .

As I finished writing this, Anthony's words resounded in my heart. *This is only the beginning*, I thought, smiling. *Tomorrow is a good day, indeed.*

Chapter 16

GOOD TRIUMPHS OVER EVIL

I was relieved. Anthony and I had made it. We were on the other side of this crazy journey, and I was simply amazed at the thought of what had taken place during the previous ten months. No human could have begun to orchestrate what God had completed. But I also knew my journey was far from over. God wasn't even close to being finished with us yet.

I was a bit overwhelmed with the whole thing, to be honest, and I cried often. But my tears were no longer tears of sadness or pain or loss; they were tears of relief and joy and excitement. Yet I have to admit, there was a little fear mixed in with all that emotion. God hadn't done this just for Anthony and me. I don't think God ever intends blessings to stop with those He blesses—blessings are intended to flow through every one of us to others. So I knew He had a plan to use this, and I desperately wanted Him to. But I didn't know what that meant for me.

I wondered how my life would change. I wondered how it would impact my family. I was a stay-at-home mommy, a committed wife, and I didn't want to leave my family to go gallivanting around from here to there to tell people all that happened. But I did want people to know—I really did—and so everywhere I went, I began to tell people my crazy story of redemption. I think I was a bit over the top at first, but I just couldn't help myself. I was just so astounded by Jesus and all He had done. I was so captivated by His love and grace and mercy that I eagerly began to shout His praise to anyone willing to listen.

I wanted all to know that Jesus is who He says He is. That He is God and that He redeems. I was living a life I never thought possible. My pain had been healed and my past redeemed. And I needed others to know that Jesus could do that for them as well. They didn't need to sit in their pain and settle for a life of mediocrity. They could be healed as I had been and could experience the life Jesus died for them to have. I wanted to be used by God. I wanted to be His instrument of grace to bring hope and healing to others.

At the same time, I was scared. I was afraid of what the next steps in my life would look like. Yet I knew my calling was to bring light to a broken and dying world, so once again I would follow.

Anthony responded quickly this time, within only a few days:

Dear Laurie,

Thank you for your last letter. The last two or three letters we had exchanged had been so hard to receive and respond to. This one I actually looked forward to. I guess once the burden was lifted so was my anxiety. God has truly blessed me through our letters. I'm glad he has blessed you too.

Speaking of that, I will be praying for you and your adoption, that it goes smoothly and that you and your husband and of course the child/children, are blessed.

. . . I still have men coming up to me and thanking me for our testimony, praise God! I know God will continue to work through us for His good purposes. This horrible tragedy has changed our lives forever. But God can use it, and I believe He will, for the rest of our lives to help others. It's kind of scary and yet exciting, isn't it?

. . . You know not only have I had to work at forgiving Diane, but your dad also. I've forgiven them both. I've never thought about anyone else needing it! I understand your family's anger and even hate. And of all the people who took the stand to testify against me, you were the least severe. But I do forgive you, that's a given, and I thank you for asking for it. You are truly a kind and Godly person, your family is very blessed to have you.

I also want to thank your husband for allowing our correspondence, that was very trusting of him. Just because I needed your address to respond, and he didn't know me. That and watching his wife go through this emotional roller coaster must have been hard. Let him know thanks.

I will be praying for you and your family and the addition you are looking forward to. Take care and God bless. If you have any more questions please write, and I'd still like to send you a picture (drawing) if you'd like.

God bless,

Anthony

Anthony was feeling God's call on his life just as much as I was, and I can't even begin to explain what joy it brought me to know that he'd be in that prison bringing the gospel to other inmates. This is what I had prayed for all along, and it was happening.

I wanted God to use our story to bring hope and healing to these men so they might find redemption and meaning in their lives. So they might be able to experience joy and all the goodness God has for every one of us in this life. I wanted to see them come to a good place, whether or not they ever stepped foot outside those walls again.

God had been changing me. My heart ached for the men in that prison. I couldn't help but think their crimes may be directly correlated to the pain they experienced earlier in their lives. Wounds that left their mark. Suffering inflicted by others that had taken its toll, contributing to the reason for their offense. Now, don't get me wrong. Whatever crime it was that brought them there was not okay. They had sinned. There's no excuse or justification for that, and every one of them needs to face the consequences of their actions. But like Anthony, there were reasons behind their actions, and I wondered if some of those reasons had to do with unresolved pain. Pain that could be healed. Redeemed. Used for good.

These men could change. I mean, isn't that the whole aim of every prison rehabilitation program? To reform inmates so they can become productive, contributing members of our society when set free? It should be the goal of every person involved in the prison system. But I don't believe any real, lasting change can come out of even the best rehabilitation program. No measure of rehab can ever transform an inmate, or anyone else for that matter. We cannot change ourselves. Change comes by the grace of God alone. True rehabilitation—true transformation—comes as we submit ourselves to God by faith in Jesus, not through some five-step program devoid of God. But I thought if God could use the powerful story He had entrusted to Anthony and me, it had potential to bring the change needed within those prison walls. We could bring light to that very dark place. This is what I wanted, this is what I prayed for, and I thanked God that He had begun to give Anthony this vision as well.

I responded to Anthony a few days later:

Dear Anthony,

I'm happy to hear that our correspondence has been a blessing to you! Early on, I prayed for that, even though at the time it was counterintuitive to how I was feeling. I now pray good for you without those contradictory feelings, which is proof of God's healing hand.

Thank you for praying for me, my family, and the adoption. We're very excited about it, and our girls are more than ecstatic to have a new baby brother or sister or possibly two.

. . . I'm still in awe, though not surprised, of what God has been doing in our lives, and what He's doing through our testimony! Continue to let Him use you in this, and I'll do the same out here. Several people have told me that I should write a book on God's grace and forgiveness pertaining to our testimony. I don't know if that's where God will lead me, but if it brings Him glory, leads people to Him, and leads them out of bondage to their unforgiveness, then it may just happen down the road if it's God's will. Certainly not now. I think there's more to our story than has already been written at this point, so I think it'd be a bit premature. Who knows, we'll see. I agree—it is kind of scary and exciting! We serve an amazing God!

. . . Thank you for recognizing Travis' (my husband) difficulties throughout all of this. He's an amazing man, and I could not ask for a better husband. I am truly blessed! It has been an emotional roller coaster, but it's been worth it. Travis and my mom, especially, had a difficult time seeing me go through this, but I've known all along, and they both trusted me, that this was God's will for me. I was and am confident that this is where God was and is leading me, and I've known that He would use it for His good purposes. All glory to Him!

If you'd like to send a picture, I'd be happy to receive it. I hope you're doing well!

Take care and God bless!!

Sincerely,

Laurie

I tried to hide my wounds both from others and myself before this whole journey began. I wanted to have it all together. I wanted to be past my pain, so I would paste a smile on my face and put on a show. I was supposed to be happy. I was supposed to be strong. And so I pretended that I was and figured if I did that long enough I might just fool myself into believing it was true. For a while, I think it worked.

But God didn't allow me to fool myself for too long. He brought my pain to the surface—He made me deal with it—so that He could bring me to a place where there was no need to pretend any longer. A place where I could retire all my happy masks for good. As my wounds surfaced, I became increasingly irritable—that's what brought me to my knees in the first place. I was ugly, and I didn't like who I had become.

Irritability became the marker of my pain and the gauge by which I could assess my healing. During my correspondence with Anthony, my irritability decreased gradually over time. It was still there, just not as intense and certainly not as noticeable. Then one day—a while after I had witnessed all God had done—I noticed it was gone.

I was going about my business as usual that day—taking care of my girls, doing laundry, and such—when it struck me that I was happy, not grumpy, and I wasn't putting on some show, as I had done so often before. It was real. I truly felt joy and, as I thought about it, I realized that I had felt that joy for a while. For some reason, I hadn't really taken notice of it until then. Maybe I wasn't aware of it right away because the irritability had gone away slowly over several months. Regardless, my irritability was gone—along with all the bitterness and anger I had held for so long.

I had changed. I wasn't the same person I was when I first began this journey, and Anthony wasn't either. The more letters I received from him, the more his transformation was confirmed. He was truly living life to the glory of God in that prison. In one of his letters, Anthony wrote, "Thank you for having reached out to me. This last year has been one of the hardest yet most gratifying experiences in my entire life. It has been an experience that has humbled me before our God. It has healed me in ways I never thought possible, praise be to God."

In another letter, he wrote, "I may not have told you this, but as we worked through our trials and letters, my hunger for God grew. You made God's forgiveness and His sacrifice on the cross very very real to me. My flame was fanned by our correspondence and the Holy Spirit. I will always remember getting your first letter and the fear I felt. But also excitement, cuz I knew God was about to do something great. And He never disappoints!"

Sometime later, he wrote, "I've got to tell you, I wonder had I not come to prison would I have stayed a fan of Jesus or become a follower. I knew Him. I went to Bible studies, I read my Bible daily, but I didn't let Him into every dark corner of my heart. I was not a follower."

Then he wrote, "Yes God will use me in here, even if I don't want to be here. But I *must* stay open to the Holy Spirit using me wherever I may be. Thank you for your words of encouragement. . . . You have been such a blessing in my life."

God had changed this man before my very eyes.

Anthony did end up sending that drawing to me. It was a picture of a pair of old spurs hanging on a barn wall. It was pretty amazing, really. Not what I expected. Anthony is a gifted artist. He wrote to me about the picture, saying, "It struck me as so lonely, just a pair of spurs hanging on a wall. It reminded me of how lonely you said you were for your dad. . . . I held onto it for the last six months hoping and praying we'd get to this point so you'd want it or at least be open to feeling it. I believe art is something we feel and while this is not an original, I have changed it and made it my own. I hope you like it. I hope it brings good feelings."

Anthony didn't have much to give. Both he and I knew there could never be any real restitution in this situation, but with this drawing, he was giving me what he could. He was giving me something of my dad. Dad never did own a pair of spurs—nor did he own a horse—but he did love all things western. Anthony knew that; so with this picture, I think he was trying to give me part of what was lost.

After I read Anthony's comment about the picture, I stared at those lonely spurs for some time, trying to sort out my feelings. I *was* lonely before, without my dad. I sort of felt like someone was always missing, and I'd always wished things had turned out differently. But I wasn't lonely anymore. I knew God had allowed Dad's death for whatever good purpose He had. I knew He would use it. And I was okay with it now.

Anthony put a lot of thought and time into that drawing, and I was thankful to him for doing that for me.

At some point, I wrote a letter to Anthony to thank him for all we had been through together:

Dear Anthony,

. . . I'm happy to hear that you have been blessed throughout our journey. I, too, have been blessed in inexplicable ways! All to the glory of God! It's been a roller coaster, for sure! Truly, at times, I didn't think I could continue, but through grace, God led me well, and I think both of us came out the other side better for it.

Thank you for your willingness to let God work. I pray that we both remain open to His leading, and allow Him to use it all now on a different level—to bring healing to others! It is my deepest desire to be an instrument of His grace, and I believe we have something unique enough here to accomplish this. . . .

While I would NEVER have hoped for or wanted or wished for any of this, I do see God using it for good. Not just in our lives, but in the lives around us! It's sad that my dad had to die for all this to happen. And I have to be honest, it sucks. It really does. But I have to accept that in God's sovereignty, He allowed it to happen. He had bigger plans, which included my dad's salvation. Plans that may just change this world, if we allow Him to use us.

Also, I would like to thank you for being so open throughout our correspondence and for being willing to dig back into a very dark part of both of our lives even though you didn't want to. Coming to that place of honesty took courage. Thank you for going there and allowing God to lead you along the path we both took. What God has worked in you (and me) is amazing. Seeing you come to a place of repentance was one of the most phenomenal events of my life. I know it wasn't easy for either of us, and we couldn't have come to this point if you hadn't allowed the Holy Spirit to work in you . . . so thank you!

. . . Anyway, I pray only the best for you. I thank you for everything. Keep that voice of yours in there!!! Don't let it fizzle out. Don't allow Satan to distract you (which is what I've noticed him doing with me) from your purpose—bringing glory to God, sharing what He's done, being a light in the darkness. . . .

Blessings,

Laurie

Our relationship had a new purpose, centered on Jesus and the calling He had for our lives. We continued writing letters of encouragement to one another, spurring each other on to glorify God through our story. Anthony wrote things like, "Keep walking with our Lord, keep writing, your words are truly inspiring." And, "I always pray for you and your family and will continue to do so till I'm standing next to our Lord. Be encouraged, God will continue to do great things through you!" And I did the same.

Anthony and I were set on the same path. We had been given the same mission with two different mission fields—one in prison and one in the world. This thing was no longer changing just us. The more we talked about what God had done, the more people's lives were impacted. It was amazing, really, watching God work like that.

Good had most definitely triumphed over evil.

Chapter 17

GRACE

Anthony and I had exchanged forty letters at this point, and I was starting to think it was time to wrap it up. I knew our story wasn't over—God was still doing some pretty amazing things with it—but I felt Anthony and I had begun a new chapter in our lives and should move on.

I didn't think we needed to continue writing back and forth so frequently. I thought it would be weird to do that. I mean, what would we write about, anyway? Our lives? That was going a bit too far, I thought. That was going past forgiveness into reconciliation, and I don't think God requires us to reconcile like He requires us to forgive. The Bible speaks about reconciliation—that we are forgiven and reconciled to God through the blood of Jesus—and God does seem to encourage us to reconcile with others whenever possible. But I don't think He requires it.

So it was time for a change—but I didn't think we'd stop writing altogether. I thought it would be a good idea to keep one another up to speed on how God was using our story. I envisioned writing once or twice a year when I had big news or something else to share with Anthony on the ministry front. Other than that, I saw no need to continue on as we had.

With that in mind, I wrote Anthony a letter, and at the end of it, I said:

. . . It seems this part of our journey is coming to an end. A chapter has closed, yet we are beginning a new one. I don't believe God is finished with this yet either, but I think it'll look different now. . . . I will write if anything big happens in regard to God using our story, so you may rejoice in seeing God at work. I hope you do the same.

You'll be in my prayers as well. . . . I pray once again for God to use you mightily right where you are!! You are in a good position to bring the light of Christ into a very dark part of the world. I hope you keep the eyes of your heart open to His leading! I wish you well.

Peace and blessings,

Laurie

I had only good in my heart toward Anthony, but this letter served as a farewell, of sorts. After I sent it, I went about my week, thinking it was pretty much over. I mean I knew God was going to use it all—He had given both of us a story to share with the world, so that part wasn't over—but I thought all the correspondence, all the frequent letters back and forth would be a thing of the past.

I was wrong.

I told both God and Anthony I'd write if anything big happened and, sure enough, something did. As I stood singing to God in worship one Sunday morning, God's call to write this book was made undeniably clear. It was time, and I knew it.

Only eighteen days after I wrote my farewell letter, I sat down to write Anthony again, telling him about what I believed God was calling me to do. I sort of chuckled to myself, as I wrote: "Bet you didn't expect to hear from me so soon, did you?!?" Of course, Anthony was surprised to hear from me, but "pleasantly so," he said. I asked for permission to use whatever I needed to tell this story and was given consent to write the book however God led, which I was thankful for.

I found it interesting that God didn't allow me to stop corresponding with Anthony. I tried. I truly did. I had every intention of putting an end to that chapter of my life. I wanted to move on. I wanted to simplify things. Continuing the correspondence seemed so complicated, and I just wanted to be done with it all. I wanted to cut ties and move on with my life. But God didn't allow that. He wasn't finished with us, and I believed with every part of my heart that God wanted me to continue to write to Anthony. So I did. We both did. As of the writing of this book, more than one hundred letters—centered on how God would have us use this story—have passed between us.

It was weird, at first—continuing to write. I remember getting a Christmas card from Anthony that year, and it seemed so strange to be getting something like that from the man who murdered my dad. I didn't know what to do with that card, nor did I know what to do with any of the other things God was calling me to in this area of my life. But as time passed—and I continued to seek Jesus with all I had for the wisdom and discernment I so desperately needed—I learned that I didn't need to know how my life would play out one or two or even ten years down the road. Proverbs 3:5–6 says, "Trust in the LORD with all your heart, and do not lean on your own understanding. In all your ways acknowledge him, and he will make straight your paths." I had come closer to living out this Scripture than ever before—not perfectly, of course, but closer. My reliance was on Jesus, as it had been throughout this whole crazy journey, so even though I didn't know where God was leading me in my relationship with Anthony, I had grown to be okay with that. This whole journey was taken one prayer at a time, and that had not changed.

Prayer by prayer, the letters continued.

Now, if you recall, I had been opposed to the idea of reconciliation. I didn't think God was calling me to it. But through our continued correspondence, it became precisely what God worked in both of us.

Reconciliation, I've learned, is intended to be a blessing. It's not directly commanded in the Bible, but God does call us to reconcile whenever possible. A reconciled relationship reflects the kind of relationship God Himself wants to have with every one of us. It's the kind of relationship that brings glory to God—the kind that is not possible apart from His grace. We are told, "If possible, so far as it depends on you, live peaceably with all" (Rom. 12:18). We are told to bear with one another, to have unity—all things pointing toward reconciliation. But I like how the Bible says "if possible," because I don't think it's always possible to reconcile. And I don't think God calls us to reconcile in every situation. I would never encourage reconciliation in situations where potential for ongoing abuse is present, and I don't think God would either—I don't think it's His desire for us to be hurt over and over again. But if both parties are repentant and changed by the grace of God, there are no grounds to refuse to reconcile. In these situations, reconciliation *is* possible by the grace of God, and I do believe we're called to it.

I didn't continue the correspondence with the intent to reconcile with Anthony, but over the course of a couple years, that's what happened. The relationship between Anthony and me is so unique—and quite frankly, bizarre—but I believe it glorifies God. It's a shining example of what God can do in a broken relationship. If you recall, throughout most of this journey, I hated the word *relationship* being applied to Anthony and me. I didn't want a relationship with this man. I remember recoiling at the very thought of it. But God created this relationship, and I think I'm okay with that now.

But I still have my moments.

I don't want to paint a pretty picture that isn't entirely truthful in an effort to tie this story up neatly. We all know that real life doesn't fit into a nice, neat little package, so I must admit that, from time to time, I still struggle with my relationship with Anthony. Don't get me wrong. My forgiveness has never wavered. I genuinely want good for Anthony and am so incredibly encouraged by the light he shines within that prison. But he still is the man who murdered my dad. And while I do not doubt God's hand in our relationship, I still have moments when I long for simplicity. But greater than my struggle is my desire to do the will of God, and so whatever that is, I will do—even if I must exchange a simple life for something a bit messier.

It's still ridiculously crazy to me that things have turned out the way they have. God has put my enemy in my life. The man I once hated is now someone who works alongside of me in my calling. At one point, Anthony wrote, "What Satan meant for evil, God had used to awaken a powerful voice for His glory. Use that voice Laurie. You will have to speak out, and He will direct your steps and your word. I encourage you to do what needs to be done to reach the lost. Don't be afraid. Our prayers are holding you up. No mortal man will stop what God has willed. Take care of yourself and your family, I will always be praying for you and yours."

As strange as it may be, Anthony tries to encourage me through his letters; he genuinely desires good for me and he holds me up in prayer. And despite all my wrestling, I am thankful for that and am able to trace God's hand in it.

About one year into my correspondence with Anthony, I found myself sitting across a small table from Pastor Ben at Starbucks. I had forgiven Anthony at this point and had witnessed God move in his heart. If you remember, Ben was the guy Anthony turned himself into the night of the murder. The guy who called the police. He was Anthony's pastor back then, and I'm pretty sure that, next to my family and maybe a few other people, he was the person most affected by my dad's death. So it wasn't surprising to me that he didn't want anything to do with Anthony.

Anthony had just sent Ben a letter telling him all we had gone through. Anthony was asking for Ben's forgiveness, but Ben was skeptical. In an e-mail sent before we met, Ben told me, "I am very guarded as to any information or changes in Tony. . . . I would appreciate hearing your journey and perspective."

This was the purpose of our meeting.

One of the first things Ben asked after we sat down was, "Are you sure you haven't been conned?" I wasn't offended by the question. I welcomed it. I thought it would be nice to have God's work confirmed by yet another person—someone outside of my church and my inner circle.

"I don't think so," I said. "But I'll let you be the judge of that."

Pastor Ben told me before this meeting that he had been asked by a prison chaplain to start a prison ministry. He said, "I got trained. Got the shots and was put on the guard list. I even toured the facility. A week before we were to start, I got info that Tony was transferred there. So I put a stop to things. Now this letter came. . . ." He had taken a two-hour course called "How Not to Be Conned," so I was curious to hear his assessment, both as a minister and as someone who had gone through prison training.

I set my binder of letters between the two of us and proceeded to tell Ben all that had happened from the beginning. He had questions, and I answered them. At the end, I asked, "So what do you think? Do you think I've been conned?"

"No," Ben said, in amazement. "God has really done this."

Ben forgave Anthony shortly after that and proceeded to reinstate his application for prison ministry. He's been ministering to Anthony and his fellow inmates almost every Saturday since that time.

The question of being conned came up again much later, while I was writing this book. An editor within the publishing industry had done research on my story online. She came across some information about Anthony's appeal and thought that the fact that Anthony was still pursuing his appeal might be an indication that he wasn't really where I thought he was. That he wasn't really repentant or transformed.

I didn't agree. I believe every one of us would appeal in that same situation. As long as an appeal is based on truth, I don't see how the pursuit of an appeal discredits either the offender's repentance or the offender's having taken full responsibility for those actions. To my understanding, Anthony's appeal did not claim that he didn't do it; the appeal was simply asking the court to make sure he had received a fair trial.

But when my literary agent questioned me, "Could it be possible that you've been conned?" I thought it might be a good idea to gather a bit more evidence to prove my case.

I called Pastor Ben. "You've spent the last three years ministering to Anthony," I said, "so what do you think? Do you still think, after all this time, that Anthony's truly transformed?"

"Yes. He's changed," Ben said.

"Why do you think that?"

"I see inmates every week," he said. "I minister to these guys. But I've never once heard another inmate explicitly admit their crime in front of other inmates. It's just not done. But I've seen Tony stand before these men many times and say, 'I murdered Rick.' He takes complete responsibility for what he did to your dad and makes no excuse for it."

Ben and I spoke a while longer before we hung up. After that, I thought about some of the words Anthony had written over the years. Stuff like, "I destroyed families with my selfishness." And "I live in a pit of my own making." And "I deserve death, but through God's grace, I live in the one environment that God's grace needs to be taught." And "I pray I am using the second chance that God has given me to help others."

The issue was once again settled in my mind.

Anthony wrote a few days later. Ben had told him what was going on, and he was upset. I think he mistakenly thought that my book wouldn't be published because of the appeal—that the publisher calling the whole thing into question was *my* publisher, when it wasn't. "I think your book is so important," he wrote. "Is my appeal going to stop it? I'm going to be honest, I don't want to die in prison; it's a lonely way to go. No one you love is there, but if you wanted, I'd drop it. I'll call you Friday between 1:00 and 1:30. You can tell me what I should do OK?"

I couldn't believe it. Anthony was willing to drop his appeal altogether if I told him to. He was willing to give up any chance of freedom to see God's kingdom move forward through our story.

When I spoke to Anthony that Friday afternoon, I said, "I would never ask you to drop your appeal. I don't think that's my place. The only thing I would have you consider is whether your appeal, as it stands now, glorifies God." I said, "If, to the best of your knowledge, your appeal contains truth, then I see no need to drop it. But if you know of any lies in there, then you might consider revising it."

"I think it's truthful," he said. "I haven't seen my appeal in years, though, so I'm going to have to ask my attorney if he can give me a copy so I can read it again, just to make sure. But I don't think there's anything in there that's not true."

"If that's the case," I said, "then I see no need to stop your appeal."

Anthony seemed relieved.

Anthony didn't expect to have a decision on his appeal for another year or so, but I think all this appeal talk was God's way of preparing him for what was to come. A few weeks later, Anthony wrote again, saying, "All our worry about my appeal is a moot point, it was turned down. There are guys here who say I still have options, but this may be where God wants me. I wish it weren't! But I can still glorify Him here."

Later, Anthony told me the only way he'll ever get out is through a pardon, and so it appears Anthony's life sentence will stand. Unless God works a miracle on his behalf, Anthony will spend the rest of his life behind bars.

"This must be hard for you," I said when I spoke to him on the phone a while later.

I was struck by his response. Merely days after being told his appeal had been denied, this man spoke to me about God's plan for his life. He was disappointed things hadn't turned out the way he'd hoped, but he accepted God's will over his own. His eyes had been opened to see a plan greater than his own freedom. A plan to reach the lost within those prison walls. And he accepted that plan. It seemed to me to be the ultimate test of Anthony's heart, and he had passed. Anthony, it seemed, was a changed man.

As unbelievable as it may be, God really did do this.

This all began with a simple, seemingly insignificant call. A call to forgive. To love my enemy. To allow God unhindered access to all the pain, bitterness, and anger in my soul. I had read account after account in Scripture of God redeeming losses. Of God healing physical, emotional, and spiritual wounds. I saw Jesus's heart toward the brokenhearted, and I believed God could do all that for me as well. I didn't want my faith to be just a belief system. I wanted it to be real. I wanted it to impact my life. I wanted it to change the way I lived. So I followed, believing wholeheartedly that God would deliver. That He would faithfully keep His promises.

And He did.

God was there throughout this whole thing. He was with me, giving me grace like I never thought possible. Whispering words of encouragement. Beckoning me to trust Him, to believe Him, to follow Him, and to just keep going. It was God who led me through this journey. It was He who strengthened me, comforted me, challenged me, and opened my eyes to truth like never before.

The result was incredible. I truly have witnessed God do the impossible. Grace has undeniably been poured out upon my life, and I am forever thankful.

Chapter 18

THE STORY CONTINUES

When my dad died, my family and I took his ashes to this beautiful spot overlooking Lake Tahoe off the Tahoe Rim Trail. Dad loved this spot. It was a secluded area in the wild with spectacular views—all characteristics of the places Dad loved best.

The two-mile hike in is no less impressive. The trail climbs up the side of the mountain high above Tahoe Meadows, through patches of forest. Willows, wildflowers, and sage speckle the terrain where tall pines are sparse. The meadow can be seen below throughout this section of trail, but as the trail ascends, Lake Tahoe becomes part of the landscape as well, over a ridge in the distance. And by the time you get to the place we took Dad—off the trail, through the forest, and into a clearing on the side of the mountain—the lake dominates the scene.

My dad had taken his dad's ashes to this very spot several years before his own death. I think he spent quite a bit of time at this place after that, which is why we decided to take him there. We thought he'd want to be where his own father was.

A few days after the funeral, twenty-seven family members took that hike to his final resting spot to say good-bye. It felt so strange, taking

Dad up there. I was out in nature, a place I had always loved to be. A place that normally brought joy and stillness to my heart. Yet I had none.

I made it a point to hike up there at least twice a year after that, usually around Father's Day and the anniversary of Dad's death. I went there to feel close to my dad—to be with him—but I always ended up wrestling through everything while there, trying to make sense of it all. "Why did this have to happen?" I'd question as I stared into the sky, tears stinging my eyes. "What's the point of this whole mess?"

I questioned just about everything up there. I'm not quite sure to whom I was talking, but I questioned nonetheless. I was confused. I didn't know what I believed. I didn't know if heaven was real or if it was all just some elaborate fairy tale concocted to make loss a bit more bearable. I wondered what had happened to my dad when he died. I wondered if he could hear me.

Every time I went up there, I sat on the same rock. It was there, on that rock, that I wrestled through my questions. It was there that I cried a thousand tears as I sat and talked to my dad, telling him all that he had missed. This was the place where I grappled with life and all its complexities—pain and loss and grief—as I struggled to understand the purpose of it all. The purpose of life and death.

And each time I sat on that rock, I saw something I couldn't quite understand.

The first time I went up there by myself, I saw an eagle through my tears. Wiping my eyes dry, I watched this magnificent bird soar throughout the sky above and in front of me for quite some time. I didn't think much of it at first, but then it happened the next time I was there. And the next time. Every time I went up to see my dad—every time I sat on that rock, trying to understand it all—an eagle appeared and stayed within my line of sight for what seemed like twenty or thirty minutes. I knew there was something to it, but I didn't understand what. I thought about my dad and his love for wildlife, and I wondered if it were possible for him to make that eagle fly. It was perplexing, really, and I never did have an answer for why that bird appeared over and over again on that mountain.

I went up to that spot faithfully for five years, but then life just sort of got in the way, and I stopped going. When I became a mom, it became increasingly difficult to find time to go up there on my own. We did go as a family one time, though. The girls were little, somewhere around one and three years old, when Travis and I packed them in their Sherpani backpacks and made the trek. It was hard going up there with them. I wanted to do it. I wanted to share this place with them, but it wasn't easy sitting on that rock with the little ones my dad never had an opportunity to meet. I felt kind of foolish saying it out loud, so I didn't, but in my heart, as I sat there with my little girls, I introduced them to my dad. I whispered into their ears, "You would have loved your grandpa, and he would have loved you."

I was brought to my knees the following year. I was given faith, and God began to make me new. Years passed—so many, in fact, that my toddlers grew up and went off to school. So much had happened in this span of time. I had become a follower of Christ and had witnessed God do some amazing things. I had seen hearts soften and lives change by the power of His Spirit. And I was a completely different person.

I'd wanted to go back to that spot for a while by that time, but I always seemed to find an excuse not to go. I didn't know why I was being resistant, but after I prayed for God to show me what my problem was, I began to see that I was afraid. The last time I had been there and every time before that, I had been a complete mess, and even though I believed that I had been healed by God, I was afraid I'd go up there and find that I really wasn't as healed as I thought I was. I was afraid this place would reveal more brokenness, more pain. But almost thirteen years to the day after my dad died, and three and a half years after all that stuff with Anthony first began, it was time to go.

As I packed the girls up for school one morning, I felt God tell me that I needed to go back to that spot. I fought with Him about it all morning, but by the time we left for school, I had my hiking boots on and my CamelBak on the seat next to me. "I'm going," I whispered to God, with a smirk. "I'm ready for whatever it is You have for me." I knew God was with me. And after I laid my rebellion aside, I was actually a little excited for what the day had in store.

My heart had done a one-eighty since I woke that morning. The moment I stepped out of my car at the trailhead, I felt alive. It was a beautiful day, the sun was shining brightly, and though I was very much grounded in reality, it felt like I was in a wonderland of sorts. Birds chirped as they busily flew from here to there, butterflies fluttered from flower to flower, and bees whizzed by my ear as I hiked up the trail toward my spot.

I was happy to be there.

Every other time I had gone up to this place, there was a heaviness to the outing, but this time was different. The burden was lifted. The grief that had led me up that mountain time and time again was gone. I wasn't led by my emotions any longer. I know it might sound silly, but when I set out on that trail, I invited Jesus to go with me—saying, "You ready? Here we go." I had learned the value of walking with God, and I didn't want to take one step on that trail, or anywhere else for that matter, without Him.

This hike had always been about my dad, about my grief, about holding on to something that could not be held. I used to go up there to spend time with Dad, but this wasn't about him anymore. When God healed me, I was finally able to let Dad go. And so this day wasn't about my dad—it was about my relationship with God.

I veered off the trail when I reached the timberline and hiked along a small ridge, through the forest over a bed of pine needles and rock, toward the place where we took Dad's ashes. I always think that place is a bit closer than it actually is and end up coming down into the wrong clearing, just east of the actual spot. It's only about a hundred yards shy of the place I intend, with only trees and brush separating the two clearings, but I really wanted to get it right this time. I thought if I stayed on the ridge a bit longer, I'd be able to drop down where I wanted to go. But as I descended off the ridge, I realized that I had gone a bit too far and ended up in a clearing slightly to the west. The actual spot was just on the other side of a hedge that I walked through.

"There it is," I said to myself, smiling as I saw the familiar rock. I stopped at the rock's base, let out a great big sigh, and closed my eyes—my smile still there. Not a moment later, I heard rustling in the brush in front of me, the very hedge I would have come through had I undershot my approach. It sounded like a larger animal, not a squirrel or anything like that. And before I knew it, as I stood wondering at the sound, out leapt a little fawn with speckled back and everything. My heart melted. "Awww," I said softly. "Well, hi there!" Yes, I talked to the deer. Tears came as our eyes met. I knew this little guy was a gift from God, sent to speak to my heart.

You see, my dad loved wildlife. He was a hunter, but more than that, he genuinely loved wild animals, deer especially. Throughout my childhood, I saw Dad's excitement when he spotted just about any type of big game. He carried binoculars in the door of his truck just in case he might be able to catch a glimpse of these animals. I have so many memories of Dad quickly pulling the truck over to the side of the road, saying, "Do you see those deer up there on that ridge?" as he pulled out his binoculars to scan the distant horizon.

So when this fawn leapt out of those bushes and stood no more than fifteen feet in front of me—in the very place that I wrestled through some of the most agonizing questions of my life, in the place that had come to encompass all that was my dad—I knew it was a gift from God. God was showing me that He was there.

The little deer and I stared at one another for a few moments. I know this is silly, but after a while, I thought, *This deer is from God. Who's to say God won't let me pet him?* Even writing that makes me laugh now. But in actuality, my line of thinking wasn't off. God is in control of all things. He's the God of the impossible—I had lived that truth—so with that in mind, I took a slow, calculated step toward the fawn, hand outstretched, and said, "Come here," as gently as I knew how. Now, I'd like to tell you that I became Snow White incarnate—that this ridiculously cute baby deer nuzzled up to me and proceeded to follow me down to the meadows to skip and frolic in the tall grass—but that's not what happened. No. Just as one would anticipate, the fawn scampered away. *Doesn't hurt to try*, I thought, laughing at my silliness.

I sat on the rock after that. I thought about the eagle and wondered if I'd see it this time. I wanted to, but I was okay if I didn't. I mean, God had already given me a deer. What more could I ask for?

I had done a lot of things on that rock, but this was the first time I prayed there. I knew God had brought me to this spot for a reason, so as I looked to the sky, I said, "Speak to me, Lord"—and then closed my eyes. A moment later, a rush of wind came upon my face. I felt God in that wind. He was there. And all I could say was "thank You." All the striving, all the wrestling, all the grappling to understand were gone. God had given me understanding. The moment I gave my life to Christ, my eyes were opened to see all that I was blind to for so many years. It turned out the wrestling I did with Anthony was my final match. My healing was complete.

I sat there with my eyes closed for some time, and when I finally opened them, it was there. The eagle. Flying right before me in the distance, just above the treetops. "Every time," I said with a smile as I gave thanks.

I thought about every time I had gone up there. I thought about seeing that eagle. I thought about all the pain I had wrestled with on that mountain. And I understood, for the first time, what I never could. God had brought me back to this spot to show me that He didn't enter my life when I became a Christian—He had been there all along, pointing me to Himself through many things, including those eagles.

God was with me. He collected my thousand tears in a bottle. When I felt so alone. When I wrestled with loss. When I struggled to understand. He was there. He was there when my parents divorced—when I struggled to be the one to keep it together. He was there when this terrible tragedy choked all beauty from my life. He was there when I was taunted by the fear that I might lose my child. And He was even there in my darkness, allowing the anxiety and depression to bring me to my knees, so I'd finally be able to receive His love.

Jesus is Immanuel—God with us.

He doesn't leave us in our pain. He sees it. He joins us in it. And He heals it.

Like many of you, my story is not one I would have chosen for myself. For many years, I found it difficult to embrace the life I found myself living. *But God*—there's that phrase! But God has opened my eyes to see the thread of grace He had been weaving throughout the fabric of my life from the beginning. He used it all. All the good. All the bad. He redeemed the unredeemable. And gave me a new song to sing.

There is purpose in our pain.

We all have wounds. I don't know what yours look like. I don't know if your pain is the result of a tragedy like mine or something else, but I don't think that matters. Pain is pain, regardless of its cause. But here's the thing: Jesus came that we might have life. Life to the full. He came to bind up the brokenhearted. To proclaim freedom to the captives. To release prisoners from their darkness. To comfort all who mourn. To bestow a crown of beauty instead of ashes, joy instead of mourning, praise instead of despair.

Jesus came to redeem.

To make us new.

God is with every one of us. He loves us. He wants to bring us to a new, better place in our lives. But in order to get there, we must choose to lay down our pride and resistance so that we are in a position to receive it. We must lay ourselves down with abandon and follow the only true source of healing and wholeness.

I never did get the chance to bring Anthony a Bible. It wasn't for lack of trying. It's just that the prison always denied every opportunity I had.

I was thinking about how this whole thing got started one day not too long ago, and I thought that perhaps I might have brought that Bible to Anthony, after all, just not in the form I expected. Maybe it wasn't about a physical Bible at all, but about living the Bible out. I wonder if when God told me, "Bring him a Bible," He actually meant, "Bring him My *Word*." I did that. By the grace of God, the Bible came to life for both Anthony and me during our correspondence. Though I didn't do it perfectly by any stretch of the imagination, I did bring Anthony the Bible in deed. And isn't that what it's all about anyway? Living this stuff out?

Still, I must confess, I believe God will provide me with an opportunity to give Anthony an actual Bible someday. This story is far from over. In a lot of ways, it's only just begun. God continues to use this story to touch lives in ways I never imagined possible.

I love that God's not finished yet. This life isn't about arriving at any particular destination. It's about the journey. He's not done with me, and He's surely not done with you, either.

There's more grace to be given. More mercy. More healing. More blessings.

And if God has done this in my life, if He can redeem something as unredeemable as murder, just imagine what He can do in yours.

Tomorrow is most certainly a good day.

Afterword

My name is Anthony Echols, inmate number 75531. I was the person who murdered Laurie's dad, Rick. Taking a life is the most selfish thing anyone can do. God gives us life; who are we to take it? When I killed Rick, I was a believer, so I knew this! But on the day I pulled the trigger, I wonder who I was and what was I thinking. How could I have gotten so out of control, so angry, as to have murdered this man? I used the affair as my excuse, but there is no excuse. I deserve this prison sentence and more, but thank God for His Son and His love because without that I would have stayed that angry person.

I came to Christ on Father's Day in 1996. There was an outdoor service at a local park. My wife and son had been attending church and asked me to go. The pastor seemed to be speaking right to me. Accepting Jesus as my Lord and Savior was an easy decision. I had prayed since I was little and believed in God, but until that day, I had never known how Jesus fit in and what salvation really was.

Changes in my life began to occur after that. I started to attend Bible study and began volunteering. Life seemed to cruise by. Three years later, my wife and I decided to build a new home. Rick was our contractor. Two months after we moved in, I began to suspect my wife and Rick's relationship had become inappropriate. I got some phone records and discovered they were calling each other every day. I confronted them. They told me they would stop talking and seeing each other, but they didn't. I believe I was so caught off guard because I thought I was doing the things my wife and God wanted, but in retrospect, I was a carnal Christian, which to me is a fancy way of saying I was selfish and self-centered. If we step out of God's will for our lives, we can't expect to be blessed.

Five months after the affair came to light, my wife filed for divorce. I was devastated. Then I became angry. I let that anger build until it exploded, and I pulled the trigger twice on a .22 caliber rifle, shooting Rick in the head. Now I had destroyed another family with my selfishness. I brought more pain to Rick's family with one selfish act than they should have had to know in an entire lifetime. And my sin brought so much shame to my family as well.

I was in jail for over two years waiting for trial. I read my Bible and prayed, but I stayed self-centered. Selfishly, I chose not to accept a plea deal and went to trial, hoping to receive a lighter sentence. The trial put Rick's family, my family, and many others through a horrible ordeal, and to top it off, I based my defense on a lie. I had convinced myself that the shooting was an accident. I didn't want to believe I had committed murder, but my anger, and nothing else, had killed Rick. In the end, this whole ordeal didn't even help me. The sentence I received was much harsher than the one offered, life without the possibility of parole.

I was sent to a maximum security prison in Ely. I was a little afraid, but soon found out if I stayed out of other people's business, I was left alone. Six years later, I arrived at Northern Nevada Correctional Center. I was back home in Carson City. It had been nine years since I had killed Rick. I received Laurie's letter less than a year later.

I remember not recognizing the return address. I opened it and read, "You may not remember me, but I'm Rick's daughter, and I want to come and visit you." *Whoa*, I thought. *Is she kidding!* Laurie stated she didn't want to yell at me, just wanted to talk. I felt who was I to deny her this, so I agreed. Ultimately though, she was denied a visit by the warden.

During the wait we started trading letters. I look back and see God's hand in this. What could have been a quick visit and possibly a half-felt "I'm sorry" or "I forgive you" turned into a two-year incredible journey.

Of course at first, I wasn't a committed participant. We had traded a few letters when Laurie told me she wanted to forgive me, but she also wanted to know what happened that day. I hadn't told anyone what actually happened that day. I didn't want to go back over it. I was satisfied with my flimsy excuses. Up to this point, I had kept God's light from shining into this area of my life. I knew going over this with Rick's daughter was going to force the door open and let God's light in. I wasn't ready for that. I wasn't ready to trust Laurie, maybe God, either. I was willing to work through forgiveness though.

The process was a slow one. Sometimes I felt so guilty about the things Laurie wrote about that I could hardly write back. But God had placed us on this path, so I kept writing.

About six months in, Laurie sent me a testimony she'd written and posted on the internet. I freaked! A lot of the information in it about me hadn't come from me. The trust I was developing for Laurie shattered. I couldn't write back for a long time.

Finally, I responded. Laurie sent a revised testimony, but I didn't like it either. At this point, I was ready to give up. Laurie couldn't visit and the letter writing wasn't getting us anywhere. Satan was about to derail us. But God was encouraging Laurie because she didn't give up. She sent me a third testimony. It was good, real good. And my trust began to return.

I still couldn't write about the day of the murder, but I began to examine it. Doesn't it seem like our worst day is also shared with someone else? Now imagine you are responsible for that worst day, yours and another's. All you want is for that day to go away, but there can't be healing if you sweep it under the rug. God doesn't set it up that way, so I dug in.

I'm not sure when I received "the letter" from Laurie, but I remember reading the words, "I forgive you. . . ." Suddenly the enormity of what I had done punched me right in the gut. Tears came, guilt threatened to overwhelm me. What had I done? How could I have done it? I had asked God these questions: How, why? And He always responded as Laurie did, "I forgive you." Had I taken His forgiveness for granted? I knew 1 John 1:9 said if we confess our sins, God is faithful to forgive us. But the cost of that forgiveness began to sink in. And how did that explain Laurie forgiving me? Yes, God's Word tells us in Matthew 6:14 that we are to forgive as we have been forgiven, but how many of us actually give it or receive it? I knew Laurie had not said these words lightly, that it was one of the hardest things she'd done. I also knew her relationship with Jesus would not allow her any other way. "I forgive you." This was sacrificial, pain-filled, forgiveness. Forgiveness the world can't understand and too many Christians won't try to give. We have to forgive though, even when it's the most counterintuitive, gut-wrenching thing we'll ever do. That is why Jesus hung on that cross: forgiveness.

With that in mind, I was finally able to put that murderous day on paper. I sent it to Laurie, knowing there would be no condemnation. Forgiveness could be complete, all was in the open. Laurie and I had traveled through our own valley of death. Out of the darkness and into the light. God had guided us; we had made it.

Most people would have expected Laurie to be done with me now. All of us have said, "I forgive them, but I can't forget. I want nothing more to do with them!" But this is the exact opposite of God's heart. God forgives us through the blood of Christ to forget what we have done so that He can reconcile us to Himself to have a relationship with us! This is the forgiveness Laurie gave me also.

Now we had a story to tell. Laurie had been doing that for a while through her blogs. She invited me to guest write for her blog, and I've done so three times. I've also shared our story here many times. Every time we have shown Laurie's testimony, men have been brought to tears, hardened criminals no less. God has even opened the door for me to speak at a victims impact class. One hundred fifty men were there, and they kept me answering questions on forgiveness for over an hour.

I've seen inmates reach out to estranged family members because of our story. My roommate (or "cellie" in prison) reconciled with his daughters after being encouraged by our story. And I know of two murders that were stopped because of our story!

Prisoners rarely receive forgiveness from those they've hurt, which in turn makes them unforgiving, but this cycle can be broken. I used the story God had given Laurie and me to not only encourage others to forgive, but to seek forgiveness with others I had hurt as well. Some have forgiven me and are part of my life. Some haven't, but I continue to pray for reconciliation.

Originally, I thought the reason Laurie and I had begun this journey was so that Laurie could have closure. I was wrong. First and foremost, I believe God had us on this journey to glorify Himself. But I also believe God intended for Laurie and me to be set free from bitterness and reflect a relationship of His forgiveness. But this journey was not easy. I know the road Laurie and I traveled was a rocky one at times. I tried her patience many times. In fact, Laurie has said before, "Forgiveness is messy," but if it wasn't, we wouldn't need a Savior who died the absolute messiest of deaths so that we could be forgiven.

God knows what's best for us. He tells us to forgive. If we don't forgive, the bitterness of every wrong will build up and infect every relationship we have. I knew this to be true. Before I started corresponding with Laurie, I was bitter. I was self-centered. I was fake. I had everyone fooled, maybe myself included. But over the first two years Laurie and I wrote, I changed. I got to see Laurie's relationship with Jesus up close. I saw in Laurie a relationship with Jesus that was humble and trusting. And I wanted my relationship with our Savior to be as intimate. I read my Bible every day, but Laurie would quote other authors as well and was always donating books to our prison library. I started reading several of them, and they helped me to draw nearer to God.

Prison is the least peaceful place on earth. But God's light shines in here also. My life did not end when I came to prison. I pray I'm using the second chance that God has given me. I too now have much to offer. Our testimony has allowed me to reach others for Christ.

So this person who was my enemy has become an inspiration and a friend. My life and my relationship with Jesus has meaning and a mission all because someone had the faith and courage to believe and put into action Christ's words, "Forgive as you have been forgiven." Separately we may never have had the impact that our journey together has given us. Genesis 50:20— "As for you, you meant evil against me, but God meant it for good, to bring it about that many people should be kept alive, as they are today"—is a verse that fits our situation to a T!

I hope and pray our story helps others find forgiveness.

Anthony

Inmate Letters

When writing the end of this book, I sent Anthony a letter asking him to jot down a quick list of all he has seen God do through our story. But instead of sending me a list, he asked if any of the men in his church would like to write down how our story has impacted them, and they did. I was surprised, humbled, and blessed to receive the following letters.

Dear Sister Laurie,

My name is Lonnie, I'm 72 years old. I've been a Christian since 1981. I've seen and heard a lot of things in 32 years as a Christian, but your testimony rocked my world. I've tried several times on the phone to describe your testimony to my son, and all I end up doing is bawling like a baby. And that's really something considering I was a hard-core biker for the first 40 years of my life. Thank you for making it [your testimony DVD].

God bless you,
Lonnie

...

Laurie's act of forgiveness has shown me one doesn't truly trust God until you trust Him to do the impossible (Matt. 19:26).

Beau

•••

Hebrews 6:10 NKJV—For God is not unjust to forget your work
and labor of love which you have shown toward His name, in that
you have ministered to the saints, and do minister.

Hello Sister Laurie,
First of all, may our Lord and Savior Jesus continue blessing
you and your family. The above scripture is for you because you
minister to our church and my heart through your DVD. I cried
seeing how God healed your heart to forgive Tony.

Those five minutes touched our lives. Personally it allowed me
to forgive a man that killed my son, that I may or may not met
before. God said vengeance is His, not mine (Rom. 12:17–21).
Your forgiveness DVD was so humbling I ask Tony to show it to
the new men in our church and speak on it! Tony and you are the
perfect example of forgiveness, and I thank God for your courage
to re-live your pain so others may be healed.

Pastor Hank
Christ Covenant Community Church

•••

I was blessed to see your [video] twice. Both times you touched
my soul. Both times as I looked around to see who was seeing
me crying I found most of the other big bad convicts were wiping
their eyes. Christ says we are to forgive others so He can forgive
us—well that takes the power of the Holy Spirit as we can't do
it. The love of Christ shines in your countenance and it humbles
me to see that your forgiveness is genuine. It has given me hope
that one day my victim will one day be able to forgive me and
allow God to heal her. I know God is proud of His little girl—you!
Thank you for your sharing—you are a brave young woman.

In His love, your brother in Christ,
Rod

•••

Hi! My name is Chuck, and Tony asked if I could write a little bit about how Lori's testimony affected me. At the time, Tony and I were cellies and I was going through some issues with my teenage daughter, whom I had not spoken to in almost sixteen years at that time. [My daughter] was under the impression that I did not want anything to do with her or my other children, and being in prison with no way to find out where they were or to get in [touch] with them lent credence to that theory. I won't go into detail, but because of some things that were going on in the house, the children were put in foster care, and foster care contacted me. I was thrilled that I might be put back in touch with my children, but was totally unprepared for the letter I receive shortly after. My daughter wrote and explained how all of my children felt I had abandoned them and that she hadn't decided if she could forgive me. I had been praying for years to be able to talk to my children, to see them grow up, to be a part of their lives, and when I am able to contact them, I find that they may not want to have anything to do with me. My first instinct was, "How do I convince my children to forgive me?" But after talking to Tony and hearing Lori's testimony, I had to realize that nothing I could say or do would make them forgive me. They had a right to be angry; so all I could do was let them know that I love them, to show them I am not the same man who came to prison so many years ago, and above all else to give everything over to God. I know that if I had pushed, cajoled, or even begged over and over again for forgiveness, I would have pushed my daughter away. God put me in that cell with Tony at a time in both our lives when Tony could minister and share with me, and at a time when the opportunity to see Lori's testimony could be such a blessing in my life that to this day, my daughter is still in touch with me, I've had an opportunity to meet her husband, and because [she] was able to forgive me, through her I may even have the opportunity to get to know my other children; to be a part of their lives, too. I just want to say thank you to Tony and Lori and to God for putting them in my life at just their right time.

...

I've known Tony E. for years and to see God's hand upon his situation has had an amazing effect on a lot of people. First to see the weight lifted from Tony and the forgiveness from his victim's family. Only the love of God can bring this about, to shine the light on our own transgressions and God's love and forgiveness of them, even death on the cross in turn allows us to share that same LOVE.

Chance

...

And above all these put on love, which binds everything together in perfect harmony. And let the peace of Christ rule in your hearts, to which indeed you were called in one body.

Colossians 3:14–15

I get to see first hand the impact of yours and Tony's story. I see men in tears, amazement, and hopeful that your story could be theirs.

I am so overjoyed that you not just talked the talk, but you walked the walk. And as I have informed Tony, this is so much bigger than you or him can imagine. God is in control, and with that being the case watch what He does!

As I write to you now my heart is so filled with anticipation of how God is going to take your story and touch the world.

And I thank you, and your family for giving to the Lord. We are lives that are forever changed by your story.

Walk in love always,
J.

...

Tony has personally changed my life. I'm here for a violent crime and came in filled with anger. I originally plotted revenge but through coming to Christ and Tony's example I have forgiven and been forgiven by my victim. Tony's example has helped me walk through this dark experience into Jesus' light.

Gregory

...

Sister Laurie,

In almost 20 years of incarceration I have seen so many inmates bitter, angry, justifying, rationalizing, and minimizing. I have also seen victims bitter, angry, scared, hateful, condemning, and maladjusted.

Seeing and hearing your video and knowing Anthony shows me that through our great awesome and loving God's divine healing power we can give and receive forgiveness resulting in healing and closure. Without this, victims stay victims and criminals stay criminals.

God bless you and your ministry.

Love in Christ,
Chuck
Ephesians 6:19–20

...

When Christ says forgive your enemies it is not for the sake of the enemy, but for one's own sake that He says so.

Laurie,
Your testimony as touch my heart and soul. I am so thankful that God as touch your heart to forgive.

Miles

...

Laurie,

Your testimony has changed my whole outlook on forgiveness
and my faith has increased three fold. With time I hope to have
as much strength as you.

God bless,
Bret

...

Dear Laurie,

Greetings in the name of the Lord Jesus Christ! Forgiveness
is something foreign to most people unless you are going
through it. The story that Tony and you share is unbelievable.
God has a way of making sure you know it's Him who's doing
something. Bringing people together is truly His business. It
inspired me to write my daughter, who is also my victim. She
wrote me right before Christmas saying she forgave me, I
answered asking specifically for her to forgive me for all that I
have done. Her brother too. I've heard from my son, and we are
getting better. I have yet to hear from my daughter, but I'm still
hoping and praying. Thank you for your story. It gives me hope,
encouragement, lifts my spirit!!! Thank you and God bless.

Sincerely,
Shawn

...

Dear Laurie,

Your testimony about forgiveness was very touching to me. My name is Richard. I am in prison for the same kind of murder as Tony, except I killed my wife and her lover. The reason why your message of forgiveness was so powerful to me is because I need to be forgiven by my four children. At this present point in time, they refuse to forgive. I know that their resistance to obey God's command to forgive is causing their lives so much pain and sorrow. They seem to believe that to forgive me would be letting me off the hook for taking their mother's life. It's been thirteen years since the crime occurred and I only have communication with one of my sons. I wish that your message could somehow reach their hearts. Please pray for my daughter and my sons. I feel that God has blessed you with a large measure of His Spirit. Thank you for manifesting a true example of Jesus for all to see. I pray that God will bless you and your family in even more special ways.

Yours in Christ,
Richard

Postscript

We are using the Bible's definition of adultery in this book. The use of the terms *adultery* and *affair*, used by either Anthony or me, is in no way an implication that a sexual or other physical relationship was going on between the parties spoken of. The biblical definition of adultery can be found in Jesus's own words, when He said, "But I say to you that everyone who looks at a woman with lustful intent has already committed adultery with her in his heart" (Matt. 5:28). This definition applies to both men and women. *The Evangelical Dictionary of Theology* states:

> In his teachings Jesus stands firmly in the traditions of the Mosaic law and prophecy by regarding adultery as sin. But he extends the definition to include any man [or woman] who lusts in his [or her] mind after another woman [or man], whether she [the woman or man being lusted after] is married or not. *It is thus unnecessary for any physical contact to take place, since the intent is already present* (Matt. 5:28).*

We have no evidence that any sexual relationship existed between my dad and Diane, and any implication to that effect should be immediately disregarded. All statements contained in this book pertaining to their relationship are based upon my opinion or the opinion of the individual being quoted.

---

*Walter A. Elwell, ed., "Immorality, Sexual" in *Evangelical Dictionary of Theology* (Grand Rapids: Baker Books, 1997), emphasis mine.

I felt so big whenever Dad let me drive our boat.

Wildflowers blanket the terrain during one of our many family hiking trips.

My family skiing at Mt. Rose with Opa.

Dad and I being silly while celebrating Thanksgiving at my aunt and uncle's house.

This is one of my favorite pictures with my parents, taken the day I graduated from high school.

Dad playing with Emily, his first grandchild, on our trip to Lake Powell weeks before he died.

Travis and I tubing on our Powell trip.

This is how I remember Dad best.

Travis and I married.

We had babies!

We have finally been matched with our two children in Ethiopia, well over four years into our adoption journey! We certainly didn't expect to be waiting this long, nor did we know just how apt this picture would be, but once again God has proven Himself faithful as we have continued to place trust in Him.

The family dressed up for Avery's "fancy" tea party.

Our most recent family picture taken with Mom and Gary.

My girls starting first and second grade. I just love these two little monkeys. This was the day God led me back up to the place we took Dad.

Lake Tahoe seen from the spot we took Dad's ashes.

All the letters written between Anthony and me over the course of four years.

The lonely old pair of spurs drawn by Anthony.

Acknowledgments

To my husband, Travis. You were there at the beginning of all this mess, and I still cannot get over the fact that you never left my side. You were my lifeline—the one who got me through my dad's death. And then again, many years later, as I plunged into darkness, you reached out your hand and held on for the ride, doing whatever it took to see me through. You and I have been on a wild ride together over the last seventeen years, and I am in awe of the man God has given to me to share my life with. Thank you for loving me through it all. For being an ever-present light during the dark chapters of my life. For encouraging me to pursue whatever it is God calls me to. For your unending patience with me as I wrote this book. For being my greatest fan. And for being the love of my life. I love you, my T.

To my Ella. You are my intuitive little thinker, and I love you more than I can say! You have influenced my faith in ways you cannot possibly know. In part, God used you to bring me to Himself. From the day you were born, I knew you were created for great things. Press into Jesus, my love. Keep your heart open to Him, and I know you will see beauty flow in and through your life. I cannot wait to see what God has in store.

To my Avery. You are my little fireball, and I can't even begin to explain how much I love you! I love your gift of compassion. It brings tears to my eyes to see your love for others and your heart for the lost and broken—a heart I strive toward myself. Keep that bright light shining by staying close to Jesus! God has big plans for you, my love. I look forward to seeing them played out in the years to come.

Ella and Avery, you both have been so patient with me as I wrote this book, and for that, I thank you. Thank you for keeping me on task, asking, "What chapter are you writing now, Momma?" every week, and for telling me, "Good job!" when I finished. I'll never forget that. I love you, girls. You bring light to my soul!

To my girls and to our children who are still in Ethiopia. I pray this book leaves a legacy of grace in each of your lives. I pray it reminds you that God works all things for good as you experience the many trials and many joys this life has to offer. But most importantly, I pray it serves as a testament to what a relationship with God looks like, spurring you on to deepen your relationship with Jesus for yourself.

To my mom, Kathy Stone. I love you, Mom. Thank you for always being there. For showing me what it looks like to selflessly love unconditionally. For being the example of the kind of mother all moms should strive to be. For helping Mark and Sheri and me with all we had to do in the aftermath of the murder. For watching my girls countless times to give me a day to write. For reading the book chapter by chapter as it was written. And for loving me so well. You are truly an inspiration to me, Mom. Thank you.

To Nicole Kelleher. You are my oldest friend. You were the one who first prayed for me. The one who began petitioning heaven on behalf of my soul, and I am convinced that none of this would have been possible apart from your prayers. Thank you for being that friend to me. For praying me into my salvation before I even knew I needed to be saved. For being the friend I know I can trust to provide a knowing, loving answer. I am so thankful for you. I love you.

To Sarah Grant. I can honestly say that my life, and this story, would not be what it is without you. You are my go-to. The one I know I can truly be myself with. There are absolutely no pretenses in our relationship, which is just so incredibly refreshing. It's rare that you find a friend with whom you can share all your thoughts and fears and doubts, knowing you'll be met with love, grace, and truth. I am so thankful

God put you in my life. Thank you for being the person I can go to for sound biblical advice and for walking through this incredibly difficult journey with me. I love you.

To T. Grant. You and Sarah are our closest friends, and Travis and I are so incredibly blessed to have you in our lives. You are a tremendous source of encouragement, and I can honestly say that God has used you countless times to bring clarity to whatever it is I'm dealing with. You are a godly man of integrity, and I always know I can count on you for sound guidance. Thank you for being in my life. For loving me and my family so well. We love you.

To Kim Laack. Thank you for the many years of support and love you've given me. For going out to lunch with me when I was at my lowest and having the courage to point me to Jesus. For being so loyal to me. For walking through this life with me. For being the first one to encourage me to write about my past. And for being my first editor. I love you, Kim. I always have. I always will.

To Taylor Laack. Our lives have been intertwined since birth, it seems, and I am so thankful to still call you friend. Thank you for your continued love and grace. For taking an interest in seeing me come to this place of redemption. For your guidance and love. For walking on this crazy journey with me. Your zeal for God and life amazes me. Thank you, Tay.

To Robb and Jenny Owen. Thank you for allowing me the opportunity to work through the whole mess of this journey week in and week out at our Bible study. For cheering me on from the sidelines. This story would not be what it is without you. I love you both.

To John and Sue Coombs. Thank you for your love and support. For loving Travis and me through all our crazy adventures. And of course, for taking the girls out to give me time to write as I neared my deadline. I love you. I truly am blessed to be your daughter-in-law.

To my brother and sister, Mark Albrecht and Sheri Albrecht. It's been a struggle for each of us. The day we lost Dad was a day that changed our lives forever, but by the grace of God we made it through. Thank you for being open to what God has done here. I pray your paths lead you to experience immeasurable grace. God is good. His promises are true, and He *will* give beauty for ashes to those who love Him.

To the Correlli family. Aunt Patsy and Uncle Rick, I can't even begin to thank you for all you've done for me throughout my life. You were like my second parents growing up. I have so many wonderful memories of our time together. Thank you for those. We have all struggled with Dad's death, and I know this has been difficult for you, but I'd like to thank you for opening your hearts to what God has done here. I am forever thankful. Josh, thank you for being a big brother to me. For "keeping your eye on me," as my mom asked you to do when I went back to school, days after the murder. And for helping me with some of the legal issues pertaining to this book. Jermo, thank you for being there for me, for accepting this journey even though it didn't always make sense to you, and for opening your heart back up to my family and me. Ricky, thank you for being such a wonderful source of light. You are laughing and smiling in every memory I have of our childhood. You have an incredible spirit about you, and I just know God has great things for you. Josh, Jermo, and Ricky, you all are more like brothers than cousins. I love you more than I can ever say.

To the rest of Dad's side of my family. We have been through entirely way too much together. We have seen things we should never have had to see. This terrible tragedy has changed all of our lives forever, but our pain will not be wasted. It has purpose beyond what we can conceive. Thank you for beginning to open your hearts toward what God is doing here. What was meant for evil, God *will* continue to use for good. I love you.

To Mom's side of my family who have showered me with love and grace. Even though I don't get the opportunity to see you often, you have always been in my heart. Thank you for all your support in this. I love you.

To Pastor Dan Frank of Grace Church in Reno, Nevada, for faithfully preaching God's Word each and every Sunday. Faith comes through hearing, and mine came through the words you spoke one fateful Sunday morning. God used you to get this whole thing started, and you will always have a special place in my heart. Thank you.

To Rick Turner, who was the first to greet me as I walked in the doors of Grace Church for the first time. I saw something different in you, Rick. You had a joy, a radiance about you that I desperately wanted. In my darkness, you were a beacon of light. A glimpse into what Jesus was offering me. Thank you for being the light of Christ in this world.

To Pastor Harvey Turner of Living Stones Church in Reno. When Living Stones planted outside of Grace, I knew God was calling me to sit under your leadership. Your faithfulness to preach the Word in power and truth astounded me. My faith grew rapidly under your preaching, and I will forever be grateful to you for that. Thank you, Harvey, for what you do. Thank you for being the one Jesus used to strengthen my faith enough to say yes to His call to forgive and love my enemy. None of this would have happened without you.

To Pastor Bobby, my counseling pastor at Living Stones who helped me through the muddled mess and helped me discern God's will throughout this entire journey. Your wisdom and insight into God's Word were simply invaluable. Just as I have said of Harvey, none of this would have been possible without you, Bobby, so thank you. You are an amazing man of God.

To my pastors at Life Church Reno—Pastor Dave Pretlove and Pastor Tom Chism—who continually help my family and me grow. Who give counsel and voice to my story. Thank you.

To Anthony, who faithfully pursued his relationship with Jesus, allowing God complete access to his heart, without which this would not have happened. And for his willingness to allow me to do whatever God has called me to do with our story. Thank you, Anthony.

To Pastor Ben Fleming of Silver Hills Church in Carson City,

Nevada. Thank you for being a source of encouragement to me to pursue my call to write and speak about this incredible story.

To Julie Gwinn, my first professional editor, who helped me reorganize my manuscript. Thank you for giving me my ah-ha moment in how to write this book.

To my agent, Jessie Kirkland of The Blythe Daniel Agency. Thank you for believing in my story. For taking a chance on a nobody with no real professional writing experience. For seeing the potential that God saw. And for your friendship.

To the Kregel team. Thank you for giving voice to this story. For working alongside of me to give birth to the vision God has given me for this book. For patiently taking the time to work through some of the more sensitive aspects to this story. I am forever thankful to you.

I am so very blessed. God has filled my life with people to support, strengthen, and grow me. But no relationship I have compares to the one I have with God. I truly am nothing apart from Jesus. And I thank God for His unfailing love and presence.

About the Author

LAURIE COOMBS is a passionate writer and speaker on the issues of forgiveness and redemption and the blessings associated with following Jesus. Her story has been featured in Billy Graham's most recent film *Heaven*, part of the *My Hope with Billy Graham* series. She writes at LaurieCoombs.org and is a featured writer and blogger for iBelieve.com and Crosswalk.com. Laurie and her husband, Travis, make their home in Nevada along with their two daughters, Ella and Avery. Together the Coombs family eagerly await the arrival of their two children from Ethiopia.

For more information about Laurie Coombs or to book her for a speaking engagement, please visit LaurieCoombs.org. And be sure to connect with her on Twitter, Facebook, and Pinterest.

Discussion Questions

Would you like to go deeper? Discussion questions for each chapter are available for your personal or small group use at LaurieCoombs.org.